D1604204

Translating THE ANTHON TRANSCRIPT

Translating The Anthon Transcript

Stan and Polly Johnson

IVORY BOOKS
Parowan, Utah

Library of Congress Cataloging-in-Publication Data

Johnson, Stanley Q. and Polly R., 1939-
Translating The Anthon Transcript / by Stanley Q. and Polly R. Johnson
p. cm.
Includes bibliographical references and index.
ISBN 1 -890558-81-8 (hardcover)

99-067933
CIP

Printed in the United States of America

10 9 8 7 6 5 4 3 2 1

We dedicate this book
to our children
their spouses
and
their children
present and future
who are indeed
grand

CONTENTS

PREFACE

We must begin by saying that we are overwhelmed that this work proceeded as it did. We are humbled by and fascinated with the conclusions that resulted from our research.

The first gleamings of this book actually began when Larry Ferguson learned of Stan's ability to read many Native American Indian writings, as well as his passion for Egyptian, and asked Stan if he could read the Anthon Transcript. Thinking it absurd, yet having his curiosity piqued, Stan enlarged his copy and began studying it.

The Anthon Transcript consists of seven lines of horizontal letters or symbols copied by Joseph Smith from gold plates and sent to scholar Charles Anthon by way of Martin Harris in 1828. Throughout the history of The Church of Jesus Christ of Latter-day Saints, the symbols from the Anthon Transcript, while having never been translated, have been used when people wanted a representation of the figures from the gold plates. The *Encyclopedia of Mormonism* states that:

> The Anthon Transcript is also important to subsequent generations as an authentic sample of characters that were inscribed on the gold plates and thus one of the few tangible evidences of their existence. (Daniel Ludlow, ed. Vol. 1 [New York: Macmillan Publishing Co., 1992], 44)

Stan painstakingly reproduced the characters in a larger form using a magnifying glass. His ability to do this accurately and with great detail certainly was enhanced by his artistic skills. The "jots and tittles" so to speak, would have been missed by those not possessing Stan's artistic training and experience.

In order to authenticate his bronze Indian sculptures, Stan did extensive research on several Native American cultures, languages, and symbols. His familiarity with these languages and symbols which include: Micmac, Maori, Navajo, Ojibwa, Kiowa, Winnebago, Hopi, Mayan, Paiute, and Moki, combined with his Egyptian studies, made some of the symbols immediately recognizable to him. Stan began making random translations, character by character, and immediately a story evolved that was familiar to us.

The translation he produced was an account of a group of people who were guided across the ocean in barges constructed according to the instructions of the Lord, carried their light with them, and were driven by great winds to a Holy Land.

I was excited and Stan was frightened. In retrospect, it seems somewhat shortsighted that it didn't occur to us that, of course, it would be a story we knew! I turned to the account in my Book of Mormon; but Stan, not wanting to compromise his translation and not yet willing to accept the possibility that it truly was the same story, refused to look at it.

Then the staggering implications began to occur to both of us. *If* these characters copied by Joseph Smith from the gold plates could be translated by someone today, *and* the translation were a story from the Book of Mormon, then it would be further "evidence" that Joseph Smith was a prophet of God. It would be further testimony that Joseph's translation from the gold plates delivered to him by the angel Moroni, which resulted in the Book of Mormon, *was* the word of God to us in these the latter days. And significantly, *if* the unique combination of Stan's knowledge of Native American and Egyptian languages enabled him to make this translation, it would be a confirmation of The Church of Jesus Christ of Latter-day Saints' claim, that the Lamanites are a remnant of the house of Israel, and the principal ancestors of the American Indians (Book of Mormon Title page and Introduction).

In the first chapter of the Book of Mormon Nephi says, "Yea, I make a record in the language of my father, which consists of the learning of the Jews and the language of the Egyptians" (1 Nephi 1:2). One thousand years later, Moroni adds:

> And now, behold, we have written this record according to our knowledge, in the characters which are called among us the reformed Egyptian, being handed down and altered by us, according to our manner of speech. And if our plates had been sufficiently large we should have written in Hebrew; but the Hebrew hath been altered by us also; and if we could have written in Hebrew, behold, ye would have had no imperfection in our record. But the Lord knoweth the things which we have written, and also that none other people knoweth our language; therefore he hath prepared means for the interpretation thereof. (Mormon 9:32)

The house of Israel had lived in Egypt as slaves, knowing Egyptian, yet keeping their Hebrew language and religious customs. The convergence of these languages into a "reformed Egyptian" while being away from Egypt is very logical. Volumes have been written on the similarities of the languages of the Native American Indians and of the Hebrew nation in form, oddities of expression, and grammatical constructions.

> Wherefore, it is an abridgment of the record of the people of Nephi, and also of the Lamanites—Written to the Lamanites, who are a remnant of the house of Israel; and also to Jew and Gentile— . . . .
>
> An abridgment taken from the Book of Ether also, which is a record of the people of Jared, who were scattered at the time the Lord confounded the language of the people, when they were building a tower to get to heaven—Which is to show unto the remnant of the House of Israel what great things the Lord hath done for their fathers; and that they may know the covenants of the Lord, that they are not cast off forever—And also to the convincing of the Jew and Gentile that JESUS is the CHRIST, the ETERNAL GOD, manifesting himself unto all nations. (Book of Mormon, Title Page)

I think it is appropriate to tell you that we (Stan and I) know, as Joseph Smith did, that the Book of Mormon is the word of God, that it is the most correct book on the earth, and that a man or woman will get closer to God by reading it and applying its principles, than through any other book in existence, no further physical evidence being necessary. Nevertheless, it is exciting when physical evidence arises which reinforces what we already know. For instance, it is interesting when Joseph Smith's critics are proven wrong in their claims that cement was not used by Native Americans (as it mentions in the Book of Mormon) because indisputable evidence in archeological findings show that not only did they use cement but that "Pre-Columbian cement was of such superb quality that it has been difficult to match" (Paul R. Chessman, *These Early Americans* [Salt Lake City: Deseret Book Company, 1974], 4).

It is certainly amazing to realize that the Hebraisms in the Book of Mormon show that an "unlearned" farm boy could not possibly have "made up" the Book of Mormon. Hebraisms, physical evidence from archeological findings which validate Joseph's translation, and evidences of Christ's being in the New World are satisfying and enlightening, yet they are not crucial in any way to our testimony of the restoration of the Gospel of Jesus Christ in its fullness in these latter days.

After laboring with his literal translation of the Anthon Transcript for months, Stan was finally ready to compare it with the account from the Book of Mormon. It was a marvelously satisfying occasion when we realized that they matched. The Anthon Transcript told a story which was indeed in the Book of Mormon. Stan's translation was the very same story, right down to the exact number of "And it came to pass" phrases—in the correct places! We were elated, yet there were still many moments when it seemed only like an incredible possibility.

I had been doing extensive research on the history of the Anthon Transcript and, surprisingly, found that a vast amount of detailed information had been written about it.

On September 22, 1994, we met with Hugh Nibley, perhaps the only man on earth whose combined knowledge of ancient Near Eastern languages, literature, archeology, culture, history, politics, Native Americans, and the Book of Mormon would enable him to critique Stan's translation. Our appointment was at Brother Nibley's BYU office. When we arrived, however, the secretary told us that Brother Nibley was at home, yet expected back after lunch and encouraged us to call him at his home. He invited us to come right over.

Brother Nibley was familiar with Stan's Egyptian and Indian research and had previously told Stan to work on an Indian-Egyptian dictionary, so this was not their first meeting. He and Stan were deeply immersed in the translation while I listened in amazement. I took notes, and we were extremely encouraged by Brother Nibley's positive remarks, a few being: "Fascinating! . . . Interesting! . . . I think you've really got something here. . . . This is what you'd expect, the oldest story of when they came to this land. . . . Very convincing; all the signs are there. . . . The time has come. . . . What a laborious work for the translation for that little thing. . . . So Hopi: 'And they did sing praises' . . . . Darned interesting. . . . Your illustrations are very good. . . . That's beautiful work! . . . Definite pattern, connecting to the Jaredite."

I interrupted part way through to tell Brother Nibley that we should leave because it was almost the time Brother Nibley's secretary said he was to be back at his office to work on facsimile #2 in the Pearl of Great Price. Brother Nibley responded, "Oh no, this is more fun!"

We left much uplifted by Brother Nibley and with a new assurance that the translation might be correct and that this information was worth sharing. Stan followed Brother Nibley's advice to use Sir Alan Gardiner's *Egyptian Grammar* over another book he was using while translating. Brother Nibley's parting remark, "I think you're on the right path, keep going," was all the encouragement we needed to continue with this book.

Quite early, the overall story was apparent, yet there remained painstaking documentation and research for both of us for several years. We worked on this every spare minute while continuing our art business in order to make a living. Stan was chosen as the Featured Artist for the "Days of '47 Western Heritage Art Show" in Salt Lake City, Utah, in July 1997. This meant that we had to fill a large room with approximately fifty of Stan's sculptures for the week-long exhibit. Stan was greatly humbled to be chosen from the forty-seven invited Utah artists. During this time Stan sculpted the Angel Moroni holding the gold plates, which of course have the Anthon Transcript characters on the top page. Stan hand-engraves them one character at a time, each statue being unique.

One of the last steps we took in completing this work was to return to Brother Nibley with the finished translation as he had requested. Stan said, "We thought we'd bring it to you and see if you thought we were on track." He was even more encouraging than he was during the first visit.

Brother Nibley replied, "On track. Oh, yes, it's remarkable! . . . You worked your head off didn't you? This is wonderful. . . . It's amazing, you're a genius!"

When Stan told Brother Nibley that he used the different Indian languages to make the translation, the enthusiastic reply was, "Oh, it's the only sane thing to do!"

The Anthon Transcript story, which we have covered in detail in this book, fulfills scripture in Isaiah:

> Words of a book that is sealed, which men deliver to one that is learned [Charles Anthon], saying, Read this, I pray thee: and he saith, I cannot; for it is sealed; And the book is delivered to him that is not learned [Joseph Smith Jr.], saying, Read this, I pray thee; and he saith, I am not learned. (Isa. 29:11-12, King James Version)

There certainly are many "learned" men who have written volumes of research on the Anthon Transcript. Many of these have been linguists, who seemingly should have been able to translate it and write this book instead of the "unlearned" sculptor and artist, Stan Johnson, and his "unlearned" wife, Polly. We did not seek to do this, feeling inadequate to the task much of the time, yet it seems to have been something we were prepared to do, without knowing why.

We apologize for any errors in this book. We don't claim to be experts. We hope that all our efforts will have been worth it if it helps even one person to know our Lord and Savior Jesus Christ in a more personal way through reading the Book of Mormon and applying the principles therein. No other book on earth –testifies more completely of Jesus Christ. Within its pages are 3,925 references to our Savior. On average, there is a reference to Him every 1.7 verses and He is referred to by 101 different titles. All this helps us know His mission and His identity more completely, enabling us to become more like Him.

We would also like you to know that we both followed Moroni's instructions in Moroni 10:3-4 in the Book of Mormon to find out for ourselves if it was the word of God to us in these latter days. We had the truthfulness of the Book of Mormon revealed to us by the power of the Holy Ghost—in a powerful way. We promise you that you will receive an answer, too, through the Holy Ghost if you are sincere and ask in the name of Jesus Christ if it is true. We bear this testimony in the name of Jesus Christ and hope that those who do not yet know for themselves the truthfulness of the Book of Mormon will read it and ask God, in prayer, if it is His word.

We want to make it clear that Stan used his familiarity with several languages to translate the Anthon Transcript. This is very different from the translating process used by the wonderful young latter-day prophet Joseph Smith who translated by the gift and power of God. We don't claim to know why we were put in this position, but it is interesting to note how often Heavenly Father uses the weak, the simple, and the "unlearned" to do His work.

STAN and POLLY JOHNSON

Parowan, Utah
October 1999

ACKNOWLEDGMENTS

Although it would be impossible to name all those who have contributed to this book, with deep gratitude, we wish to mention a few. We thank Larry Ferguson for thinking Stan might be able to translate the Anthon Transcript and planting that seed in our mind. In 1994, when this book was just a gleam in our eye, Dale Slade gave invaluable help with the technical end of our first computer, receiving many desperate calls for assistance. Although he lives in Blanding, he made numerous trips to Salt Lake City retrieving parts for us, and spent many, many hours and dollars resurrecting our dead computer. As the deadline for publishing was imminent, Dale again stepped in to help get the book to press. Several years ago, when Stan was working on an Indian/Egyptian dictionary, Steve Kelle taught him how to do his illustrations on a computer. This was such an advantage to Stan when he started to illustrate this book. As the work progressed, we needed a Macintosh for our QuarkXPress publishing program and wonderful new friends, Pete and Margie Peterson, came to the rescue. They had purchased some of Stan's bronze sculptures and upon learning of our book, not only furnished a complete set-up with a large screen monitor, but walked us through every step of its use and told us to call anytime for assistance. Glenn Halterman, the editor of the Southern Utah University *Journal* came on board in 1999, helping us with the lay-out as well as grammatical and technical decisions. His editing expertise was invaluable. He also taught Stan how to use the QuarkXPress program more efficiently, while keeping the atmosphere "light" with his good natured wit, when deadlines loomed about us. When Glenn left to attend J. Reuben Clark Law School at Brigham Young University in Provo, Utah, our dear friend Suzette Jerolamon sat side by side with me going through the entire text *again*, and *again*, using Don Norton's suggested corrections to guide us. When the final manuscript was 99% prepared, we received a call from Ron and Chris Utter, who sweetly and convincingly gave some much needed direction in helping us to finalize the book.

There is a saying about not being able to take another's place on the wall (referring to those making a last stand on the wall of the Alamo), yet how we can stand afar and yell encouragement to those in the heat of the battle. We would like to thank some people who helped us in various ways through the years, always adding their faith to our endeavors, "yelling encouragement" to us in their own special ways: our mothers Mildred Argyle Johnson, and Johan Kennedy Gatzman, Hugh Nibley, James and Edith Goodman, Doug and Janice Andersen, Rose Thole, Ed and Mary Ballard, Jodee Packer, Dale and Donna Slade, James Reimschiissel, Clarke Woodger, Harold Ethington, David Elwess, Howard Long, Fred Oliver, Clark Powell, Steve and Jean Clay, Ben and Sandy Lloyd, Bishop Nik McOmber and Rosalie, Dianne Shafer Walker, Bob Arbon, Joe and Shirley Venus, Larry and Phyllis Haynes, Bud and Betty Halterman, Kim Whitehead, Roger and Lynette Baker, Carol Wright, David Nemelka, Maureen McCullough, Paul Milikan, Eleanor Reams, Greg and Carleen Taylor, Gwen Smith, Bishop Bill Francom, Bishop Douglas Vincent and Donnette, and Kyle Vincent.

We're especially thankful to Ivory and Cole, who still live at home, for their understanding and patience when deadlines for the book temporarily took precedence over other activities.

THE BOOK OF MORMON

In order to understand the importance of the Anthon Transcript, it is necessary to have some knowledge of the Book of Mormon and how it came into being.

The Book of Mormon is a volume of holy scripture. It is a record of God's dealings with the inhabitants of America in ancient times, and contains the fullness of the everlasting gospel. The book was written by several ancient prophets by the spirit of prophecy and revelation. A prophet-historian named Mormon quoted and abridged the words these prophets had written on gold plates. An account of two great civilizations is recorded. One came from Jerusalem in 600 B.C. and later separated into the nations known as the Nephites and Lamanites. The other, which came much earlier, is known as the Jaredites. This second group came at the time when the Lord confounded the tongues at the Tower of Babel (around 3000 B.C., according to John L. Sorenson in his book *An Ancient American Setting For The Book Of Mormon* [Salt Lake City: Deseret Book Company, 1985], 116). After thousands of years only the Lamanites remained, the rest being destroyed. The introduction to the Book of Mormon says, "They [Lamanites] are the principal ancestors of the American Indians."

This is the reason, we believe, that Stan was able to use his knowledge of Indian languages to translate the Anthon Transcript.

After Mormon finished his writings, he gave them to his son, Moroni, who added a few of his own writings and then hid the plates in the Hill Cumorah. This same Moroni, about 1400 years later, on September 21, 1823, appeared to Joseph Smith as a glorified, resurrected being.

He instructed Joseph concerning this ancient record and its eventual translation into the English language. The next day, Joseph went to the place shown to him by the Angel Moroni and saw the plates. Joseph said, "The box in which they [the gold plates] lay was formed by laying stones together in some kind of cement."

He was told by the Angel Moroni that it would be four years before he would be able to bring them forth. Four years later, on September 22, 1827, Moroni delivered the plates to Joseph. From that time forward, Joseph was severely persecuted. Joseph said:

> In the midst of our afflictions we found a friend in a gentleman by the name of Martin Harris, who came to us and gave me fifty dollars to assist us on our journey.
>
> Immediately after my arrival there [Harmony, Pennsylvania] I commenced copying the characters off the plates. I copied a considerable number of them, and by means of the Urim and Thummim I translated some of them, which I did between the time I arrived at the house of my wife's father, in the month of December, and the February following. (Joseph Smith History, 56)

It was during this time that what became known as the "Anthon Transcript" was copied from the plates.

Joseph described the plates in great detail:

> These records were engraven on plates which had the appearance of gold, each plate was six inches wide and eight inches long and not quite so thick as common tin. They were filled with engravings in Egyptian characters and bound together in a volume as the leaves of a book, with three rings running through the whole. The volume was something near six inches in thickness, a part of which was sealed. The characters on the unsealed part were small and beautifully engraved. The whole bulk exhibited many marks of antiquity in its construction and much skill in the art of engraving. With the records was found a curious instrument, which the ancients called 'Urim and Thummim,' which consisted of two transparent stones set in the

> rim of a bow fastened to a breast plate. Through the medium of the Urim and Thummim I translated the record by the gift and power of God. (*Mill. Star* 19: 118; *Hist. of Church* 4:537)

This very account makes it easy to compare these claims with archeological findings in the ensuing years, such as the following:

> More than one hundred years after the publication of the Book of Mormon, . . . the engraved metal plates of Darius the Great, [were] found where they were buried in the sixth century before Christ, in cemented boxes in the corners of the audience palace at Persepolis.
>
> It is now indisputable that engraved plates made of a hard alloy of gold were used many centuries before Christ for perpetuation of important records. And it is settled that such engraved plates, sealed in cemented boxes and committed to the earth, may remain easily legible after the lapse of more that twenty-five centuries. (Ariel L. Crowley, *The Improvement Era*, March 1942, 150)

Many critics claimed that cement wasn't used by Native Americans, as is spoken of in the Book of Mormon. "And there being but little timber . . . the people . . . became exceedingly expert in the working of cement" (Helaman 3:7). Now archeological findings show that not only did they use cement, but that "Pre-Columbian cement was of such superb quality that it has been difficult to match" (Paul R. Chessman, *These Early Americans*, 4).

The Prophet Joseph Smith Jr. said he found gold plates buried in a stone box held together with cement and was chided as an unsophisticated hoaxer. He declared that these metal plates, which had been buried for centuries, contained a religious record engraved upon them. In our scriptures we have references to Hebrew history (religious records) inscribed on metal plates, "And they made the plate of the holy crown of pure gold, and wrote upon it a writing, like to the engravings of a signet, HOLINESS TO THE LORD" (Exodus 39:30); and "The sin of Judah is written with a pen of iron, and with the point of a diamond; it is graven upon the tablet of their heart" (Jeremiah 17:1).

Referring to these two passages, Elder J. M. Sjodahl concluded, "That proves beyond a question that the Israelites were familiar with engraved tablets, for otherwise the words of the prophet would have been unintelligible to them" (John A. Widtsoe and Franklin S. Harris, Jr., *Seven Claims of the Book of Mormon* [Independence: Zion's Printing and Publishing, 1937] 33-34).

Joseph produced a transcript of characters copied from the gold plates which are left to be examined today—even the Anthon Transcript. The very things which were said by many sophisticated men to be evidences of the falsity of the Book of Mormon have been demonstrated to prove its validity. In light of modern archeological and philological finds, we know of the accuracy of Joseph's claims that ancient records were recorded and preserved in just the way he said they were!

We testify that the Book of Mormon is the word of God to us in these latter days, and that a person will get closer to God by reading it than through any other book. It boldly testifies of Christ, referring to Him 3,925 times, on the average of once every 1.7 verses. By reading it, we can know who He is in a more personal, intimate, and powerful way. He is referred to by 101 different titles, which help us know His mission and identity more completely, that we may more fully understand His ways, that we may be able to become more like Him. Some of His titles are Savior, Creator, Lord, Redeemer, Jehovah, Mediator, King of Kings, Light of the World, Second Comforter, Immanuel, Firstborn, Only Begotten Son, Brother, and Friend. How wonderful to know of His great power and majesty, to know He has the power and desire to save us from our sins if we will repent, yet also know He is our Brother and Friend. What a privilege to have the Book of Mormon, translated by the gift and power of God by Joseph Smith Jr., to guide us safely back to our

Heavenly Father and His son Jesus Christ!

We believe that the world will be judged from the teachings of the Bible *and* the Book of Mormon. Ezekiel 37:15-17 reads:

> The word of the Lord came again unto me, saying, Moreover, thou son of man, take thee one stick, and write upon it, For Judah, and for the children of Israel his companions: then take another stick, and write upon it, For Joseph, the stick of Ephraim, and for all the house of Israel his companions: And join them one to another into one stick; and they shall become one in thine hand.

The "stick," commonly used in Ezekiel's day, was a type of wooden writing tablet. We believe that each of the sticks represent a scripture; the Bible is the stick of Judah, and the Book of Mormon is the stick of Ephraim.

The Nephite scripture, or stick of Ephraim, is the record of the descendants of Joseph (who was sold into Egypt) when they were on the American continent. Elder Boyd K. Packer, of the Quorum of the Twelve, said:

> The stick or record of Judah—the Old Testament and the New Testament—and the stick or record of Ephraim—the Book of Mormon, which is another testament of Jesus Christ—are now woven together in such a way that as you pore over one you are drawn to the other; as you learn from one you are enlightened by the other. They are indeed one in our hands. Ezekiel's prophecy now stands fulfilled. (Conference Report, Oct. 1982, 75; *Ensign*, Nov. 1982, 53)

In 2 Nephi 29:10-13, the Lord says:

> Wherefore, because that ye have a Bible ye need not suppose that it contains all my words; neither need ye suppose that I have not caused more to be written. For I command all men, both in the east and in the west, and in the north, and in the south, and in the islands of the sea, that they shall write the words which I speak unto them; for out of the books which shall be written I will judge the world, every man according to their works, according to that which is written. For behold, I shall speak unto the Jews and they shall also speak unto the Nephites and they shall write it; and I shall also speak unto the other tribes of the house of Israel, which I have led away, and they shall write it; and I shall also speak unto all nations of the earth and they shall write it. And it shall come to pass that the Jews shall have the words of the Nephites, and the Nephites shall have the words of the Jews; and the Nephites and the Jews shall have the words of the lost tribes of Israel; and the lost tribes of Israel shall have the words of the Nephites and the Jews.

And in 1 Nephi 13:40, the Lord added:

> These last records, which thou hast seen among the Gentiles, shall establish the truth of the first, which are of the twelve apostles of the Lamb, and shall make known the plain and precious things which have been taken away from them; and shall make known to all kindreds, tongues, and people, that the Lamb of God is the Son of the Eternal Father, and the Savior of the world; and that all men must come unto him or they cannot be saved.

On April 7, 1829, Joseph commenced "by the gift and power of God" to translate the Book of Mormon with Oliver Cowdery as his scribe. As Robert K. Dellenbach of the Seventy in the April 1995 Semi-Annual General Conference of The Church Of Jesus Christ of Latter-day Saints commented:

> Once Joseph was free to dedicate his entire effort to translation, the work surged forward and he translated eight to ten pages a day, completing the preponderance of the Book of Mormon translation in approximately sixty-three working days" (see John W. Welch and Tim Rathbone, "The Translation of the Book of Mormon: Basic Historical Information," Provo, Utah: F.A.R.M.S., 1986, 14).

The first publication was in 1830. As of April 1995, there were seventy-three million books in distribution. Elder Dellenbach also reported, "The Book of Mormon is printed in over eighty

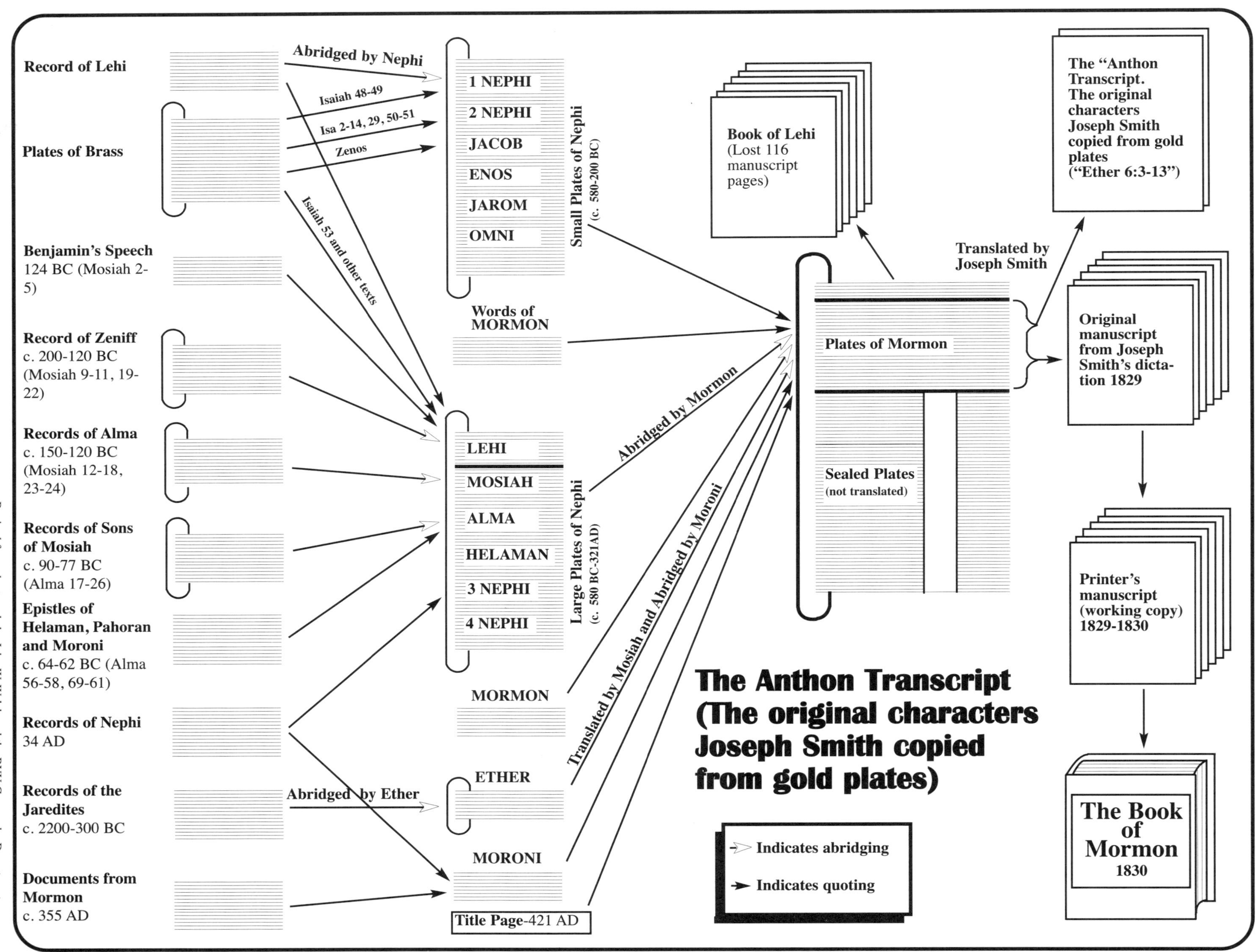

Revised from chart made by John W. Welch and the BYU Geography Department

languages and is being translated or prepared for publication in many, many more."

We love the Book of Mormon. We have read it from cover to cover many times, and continue to read it regularly with our children year after year. It presents the doctrine of Jesus Christ in simple and plain language. With all our hearts we encourage you to read and study it. We boldly agree with the words of the Prophet Ezra Taft Benson:

> There is power in the book [of Mormon] which will begin to flow into your lives the moment you begin a serious study of the book. You will find greater power to resist temptation. You will find the power to avoid deception. You will find the power to stay on the strait and narrow path. (*Ensign*, Nov. 1986, 7)

THE LORD HAS SAID:

> Thou fool, that shall say: A Bible, we have got a Bible, and we need no more Bible. (2 Nephi 29:6)
>
> Wherefore murmur ye, because that ye shall receive more of my word? . . . Know ye not that the testimony of two nations is a witness unto you that I am God, that I remember one nation like unto another? And when the two nations shall run together the testimony of the two nations shall run together. (2 Nephi 29:8)

The Book of Mormon is *another* testament of Jesus Christ!

We would like to join Moroni in saying to you:

> Behold, I would exhort you that when ye shall read these things [the Book of Mormon], if it be wisdom in God that ye should read them, that ye would remember how merciful the Lord hath been unto the children of men, from the creation of Adam even down until the time that ye shall receive these things, and ponder it in your hearts.
>
> And when ye shall receive these things, I would exhort you that ye would ask God, the Eternal Father, in the name of Christ, if these things are not true; and if ye shall ask with a sincere heart, with real intent, having faith in Christ, he will manifest the truth of it unto you, by the power of the Holy Ghost. (Moroni 10:3-4)

We have asked God, and *know* by the power of the Holy Ghost that the Book of Mormon *is* His word to us in these latter days. Reading it will help you find the *power* to be good. It will help everyone who reads it with a sincere heart, to know, revere, love, and come unto Christ. We bear this witness to you in the name of Jesus Christ.

BOOK OF MORMON LANGUAGE

The key to Stan's being able to translate the Anthon Transcript has everything to do with the evolution of Book of Mormon language from 600 B.C. to the present.

In the second verse of the Book of Mormon Nephi stated, "Yea, I make a record in the language of my father, which consists of the learning of the Jews and the language of the Egyptians" (I Nephi 1:2). The language of Nephi's father, the "learning of the Jews," was Hebrew, and the language of the Egyptians was, of course, Egyptian. We know that Nephi's father, Lehi, who lived in Jerusalem, knew Egyptian, because King Benjamin recorded (about 130 B.C.):

> For it were not possible that our father, Lehi, could have remembered all these things, to have taught them to his children, except it were for the help of these plates; for he having been taught in the language of the Egyptians therefore he could read these engravings, and teach them to his children. (Mosiah 1:4)

The *Encyclopedia of Mormonism* states:

> Written characters were handed down and altered according to Nephite speech (Mormon 9:32). This observation suggests that at least later generations of Nephites used Egyptian characters to write their contemporary spoken language, an altered form of Hebrew. It is extremely unlikely that a people isolated from simultaneous contact with the two languages could have maintained a conversational distinction between, and fluency in, the languages over a thousand-year period. Thus, if Egyptian characters were altered as the living languages changed, then the Nephites were probably using such characters to write their spoken language which was largely Hebrew. The fact that the Nephites had 'altered' the Egyptian characters according to their 'manner of speech' underscores the probability that they were writing Hebrew with Egyptian characters. In addition, Moroni's language (c. 400 A.D.) was probably different enough from that of Lehi (c. 600 B.C.) that reading Lehi's language may have required as much study in Moroni's day as Old English requires of modern English-speaking people. (Vol. 1, 180)

In Mormon 9:34, Moroni recorded:

> But the Lord knoweth the things which we have written, and also that none other people knoweth our language; and because that none other people knoweth our language, therefore he hath prepared means for the interpretation thereof."

In the period from 600 B.C. to 400 A.D., their written language had changed from Egyptian to "reformed" Egyptian.

So how did Stan correlate the Egyptian/Hebrew with the North American Indian languages which had evolved from them? It came about because of his insatiable appetite and curiosity for studying these languages. As part of Stan's research for his bronze Native American sculptures, he studied many of their signs and symbols. He attended a "Ramses II: The Pharaoh and His Time," exhibit hosted by Brigham Young University in 1985. The last day of the exhibit Hugh Nibley was invited to give a seminar on the exhibit. A slide of an ancient Egyptian text was projected on a large screen and Dr. Nibley read and translated the Egyptian heiroglyphics for the audience. The symbols looked very familiar to Stan, who had no knowledge of Egyptian at that time. He started going a little ahead of Dr. Nibley, picking out symbols which resembled Native American signs he had been studying. He was shocked to realize that on these his translation and Dr. Nibley's were the same!

Stan excitedly began an extensive study of Egyptian, finding over 200 signs which were exactly alike in Egyptian and Native American. His Egyptian helped him read the Native American signs and vice-versa.

Could it be that this unique combination of Native American and Egyptian language study was the key to the "Anthon's" eventual translation? Garcia, the Spanish historian and ethnologist, who in his day studied the archeology of America as thoroughly as any of the writers said, "Similarity in character, dress religion, . . . and customs convince me that the [early] Americans are of Jewish origin. There do actually exist many Hebraic traces in the [Native] American languages." Anthony W. Ivins, in a Conference Report, said of Garcia's conclusions:

> So this man finds that in the languages of the natives of this continent there are many traces of the Hebrew. Lord Kingsborough, who probably wrote more exhaustively on this subject than did any other historian, says, 'The Indian dialects have much in common with the Hebrew language.'

Ivins, goes on to say:

> The Indian language and dialects appear to have the very idiom and genius of Hebrew. Their words and sentences are expressive, concise, emphatic, sonorous and bold; and often, both in letters and signification, are synonymous with the Hebrew language. I call attention to these facts . . . to show you that men who have investigated this question, almost without exception, reach the conclusion that there is a very strong affinity and similarity, which leads investigators to the conclusion—many of them to the definite conclusion—that *the present inhabitants of the American continent, that is, the natives of the country, were of Jewish origin.* (Anthony W. Ivins, Conference Report, April 1909, 59, emphasis added)

Many studies have been done on the percentage of different languages found in the "Anthon" characters. The Native American Indians *are* the descendants of the Book of Mormon people. Their Hebrew language, written in Egyptian, has obviously evolved in the ensuing 1600 years, but there is enough resemblance to the original characters from the gold plates for Stan to have made a literal translation.

We enjoyed the following quote:

> It would seem to be a relatively simple procedure to compare what we have [The Anthon Transcript] with the numerous existing Egyptian dictionaries and other scholarly works of linguists and Egyptologists to see if resemblances occur. One wonders almost why it hasn't been done before. (*Improvement Era*, January 1942, 15)

We would like to reinforce our premise with a story told by Ariel L. Crowley, concerning a trip made by Doctor William Matthew Flinders Petrie and his wife, who went into the Sinai wilderness in 1904-1905 to recover hieroglyphic inscriptions. "At Serabit, Mrs. Petrie, by the merest of chance, noticed near an ancient Egyptian mine a fragment of rock with writing on it which neither she nor her husband could immediately identify."

Doctor Petrie and his men proceeded to make a careful search for additional texts in the same characters. Eight tablets were found which resembled Egyptian round-headed tablets. He was unable to recognize the characters immediately as being written in the Egyptian known to him, although Doctor Petrie concluded that he had found "a definite system, not merely a scribbling made in ignorant imitation of Egyptian writing," and dated the writing at least as far back as the time of Moses. He said these finds:

> . . . finally disprove the hypothesis that the Israelites, who came through this region into Egypt and passed back again, could not have used writing. . . . Here we have common Syrian laborers possessing a script which

other Semitic peoples of this region must be credited with knowing.

Doctor Petrie's finds remained almost unnoticed until 1916, when Doctor Alan H. Gardiner proposed the theory that these inscriptions indicated a pictorial alphabet built on the principle of acrophony, which was the missing link between the Egyptian hieroglyphs and the Phoenician alphabets. He stated:

> Out of the whole mass of commentary has grown the definite, fixed conclusion that the characters of the Serabit inscriptions are Egyptian in form and Semitic in meaning, thus inseparably linking, at a remote time, the Egyptian and Hebrew scripts. . . .
>
> The Serabit Inscriptions are closely parallel to the characters of the Anthon Transcript. . . .
>
> A great many years ago the profoundly learned Egyptologist, Heinrich Brugsch, prophesied in the introduction to his monumental dictionary that some day philological science would be astonished at the closeness of the relationship between the Egyptian and Semitic languages. The universality with which this relationship is now acknowledged may be summarily indicated by reference to a few of the major works. From the early works of Wall and Foster premised on wholly insufficient material, but tending in the same direction, to the works of Gardiner, Erman, and their colleagues and the Budge *Dictionary*, there are dissents on particular points but scarcely a serious dissent to the proposition that the Egyptian and Hebrew are akin. And all are agreed that the relationship is as of remote date certainly no later than the times of Moses.

Linda Schelle, who coincidentally is also an artist, and not a formally trained linguist, became one of the world's leading translators of the Maya heiroglyphs writing several books on the subject. She was a professor of Art History at the University of Alabama, before taking a life-changing trip down the Palenque River in 1970. In her studies, she found many similarities between the Maya and Egyptian languages.

Professor Le Plongeon spent 15 years of his life in Yucatan, exploring ruined cities, studying the language of the people, and attempting to decipher the inscriptions which he found in abundance on the walls of those great temples. After those 15 years of exploration, study and investigation, he concluded that the Maya hieratic alphabet he discovered had many similarities to the ancient hieratic alphabet of the Egyptians, saying, "The Mayas and Egyptians either learned the art of writing from the same masters, or the Mayas learned it from the Egyptians" (Anthony W. Irvins, Conference Report, April 1909, 60).

Doctor Hugh Nibley wrote:

> Instead of punctuation the original manuscript of the Book of Mormon divides up its phrases by introducing each by an 'and,' 'behold,' 'now,' or 'It came to pass.' Simply outrageous as English literature, but it is standard Egyptian practice.

The multitudinous examples of Hebraisms in the Book of Mormon demonstrate the Hebrew influence therein. One day while I was teaching seminary at Mt. View Senior Seminary in Orem, Utah, I was fortunate to observe some seminary teachers who had traveled to Jerusalem putting on a wonderful demonstration of Hebrew traditions for the students. They also gave each student a sheet titled "Other Evidences of The Book of Mormon, Hebrew Literary Styles." They listed chiasms (inverted repetitions) in Mosiah 5:10-12, Alma 36, and 1 Nephi; quasids (comparisons of people to physical features), as in 1 Nephi 2:9-10: "He spake unto Laman, saying: O that thou mightest be like unto this river, continually running into the fountain of all righteousness!" Also listed was the Semitic custom of saying "rivers" (meaning a dry river bed) versus "rivers of water" (meaning a river with water). Joseph Smith had no knowledge of Hebrew customs, what convincing evidence that he didn't write the Book of Mormon.

Why would Book of Mormon people not have written their records in their own spoken language of Hebrew? In Mormon 9:32-33 Moroni wrote:

> We have written this record . . . in the characters which are called among us the reformed Egyptian, being handed down and altered by us, according to our manner of speech. And if our plates had been sufficiently large we should have written in Hebrew . . . and if we could have written in Hebrew, behold, ye would have had no imperfection in our record.

It is apparent that it was the economy of the plates which necessitated the use of Egyptian.

The Book of Mormon Student Manual sheds light on why the plates were not written in Hebrew:

> Moroni stated (vs. 33) that if the plates had been larger they would have been written in Hebrew and therefore the record would have been without imperfection. This suggests that reformed Egyptian must not have been as capable of precision and accuracy of expression as Hebrew. It also suggests that it must have required less space to write reformed Egyptian than to write Hebrew. This helps us to better appreciate just how efficient the reformed Egyptian must have been. Compared to English and many other western languages, Hebrew is very compact. A typical English sentence of fifteen words will often translate into seven to ten Hebrew words" (Religion 121-122, Book of Mormon Student Manual, 13-14).

On page 14 of the above mentioned student manual, an example is shown of how compact Hebrew can be, using the translation of 2 Nephi 5:20 through 2 Nephi 11:3, a section that takes "nearly fifteen pages in the English version." It is written in Hebrew in this size זיחותֶסרקפּמלֹ and covers an area of about six and one-fourth inches by six and one-half inches. It goes on to say that obviously the characters are smaller than usual, however, and that:

> . . . even if one tripled the size of the characters, they would still occupy only about two pages, compared to fifteen. We have no indication of what size characters Mormon and Moroni wrote, but obviously if they rejected Hebrew because the plates were not 'sufficiently large' (Mormon 9:33), then reformed Egyptian must have been a language remarkable for its ability to convey much information with few words.

The above facts also help us understand the premise that "there are too few characters on the Anthon Transcript for them to make connected thought" is incorrect. According to Stan's findings, the seven lines in the Anthon Transcript, consisting of 213 characters, translate into 11 verses and 468 words in Joseph Smith's translation in the Book of Mormon.

In 1830, when the Book of Mormon was first published, it declared an affinity between the Egyptian and Semitic tongues which dated back to the time of Moses. "Yea, I make a record in the language of my father, which consists of the learning of the Jews and the language of the Egyptians" (1 Nephi 1:2). At that time, this was an extrordinary claim. Today, modern archeological finds and numerous scholars have proven its accuracy. Truth certainly has asserted itself out of the dust! The young prophet, Joseph Smith, even produced a transcript of characters for us to examine—the Anthon Transcript! The characters have been examined time and time again and the findings are testimony of the truthfulness of the claims of Joseph Smith and the claims of the Book of Mormon, that the Native Americans are truly the descendants of Book of Mormon people.

The translation of the Anthon Transcript by Stan, using the combination of his Native American and Egyptian linguistuc studies, is further evidence of these claims!

Along with Hebrew, their native tongue, Lehi and his children were fluent in the Egyptian Hieroglyphic and Egyptian Hieratic

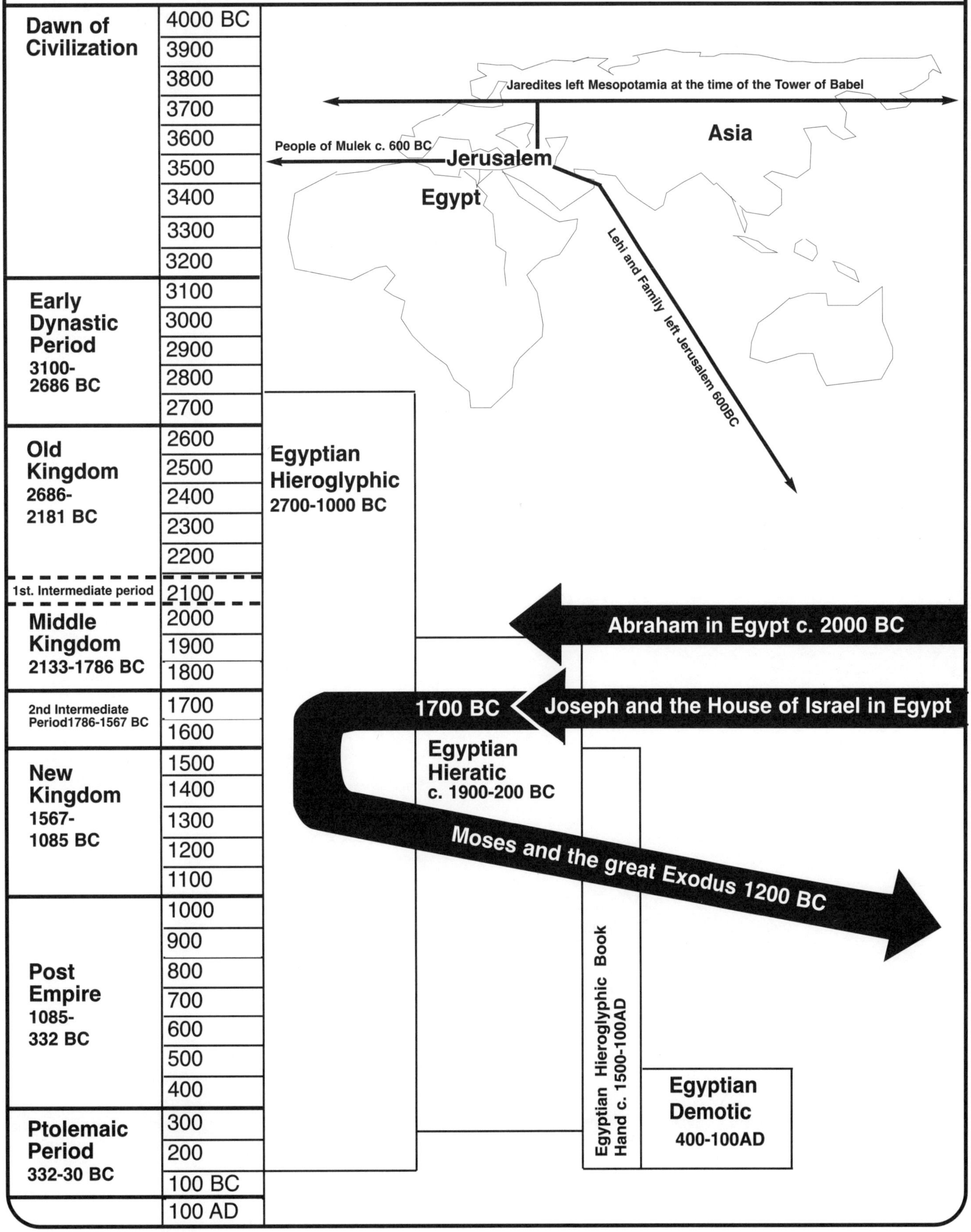

Dawn of Civilization	4000 BC
	3900
	3800
	3700
	3600
	3500
	3400
	3300
	3200
Early Dynastic Period 3100-2686 BC	3100
	3000
	2900
	2800
	2700
Old Kingdom 2686-2181 BC	2600
	2500
	2400
	2300
	2200
1st. Intermediate period	2100
Middle Kingdom 2133-1786 BC	2000
	1900
	1800
2nd Intermediate Period1786-1567 BC	1700
	1600
New Kingdom 1567-1085 BC	1500
	1400
	1300
	1200
	1100
Post Empire 1085-332 BC	1000
	900
	800
	700
	600
	500
	400
Ptolemaic Period 332-30 BC	300
	200
	100 BC
	100 AD

Jaredites left Mesopotamia at the time of the Tower of Babel

Asia

People of Mulek c. 600 BC

Jerusalem

Egypt

Lehi and Family left Jerusalem 600BC

Egyptian Hieroglyphic 2700-1000 BC

Abraham in Egypt c. 2000 BC

1700 BC

Joseph and the House of Israel in Egypt

Egyptian Hieratic c. 1900-200 BC

Moses and the great Exodus 1200 BC

Egyptian Hieroglyphic Book Hand c. 1500-100AD

Egyptian Demotic 400-100AD

EGYPTIAN HIEROGLYPHICS AND THEIR CURSIVE EQUIVALENTS

"Hieroglyphic inscriptions consist of rows of miniature pictures arranged in vertical columns or horizontal lines" (Sir Alan Gardiner, *Egyptian Grammar* [Oxford: Griffith Institute, 1976], 25).

"These columns or lines, as well as the individual signs within them, read usually from right to left, but more seldom, and then only for special reasons, from left to right" (ibid.).

"Hieroglyphic writing, in the course of time, evolved in Ancient Egypt. Out of hieroglyphic sprang a more cursive writing known to us as hieratic, . . ." (ibid., 9).

"Hieratic, so called because in the Graeco-Roman age it was the usual script employed by the priests (Greek *hieratikos* 'priestly'), is the name now given to all the earlier styles of writing cursive enough for the original pictorial forms of the signs to be no longer clearly recognizable" (ibid., 10).

Hieroglyphic Book Hand Egyptian is an impression of the formal hieroglyphic and was utilized as an informal, time-saving technique on papyri.

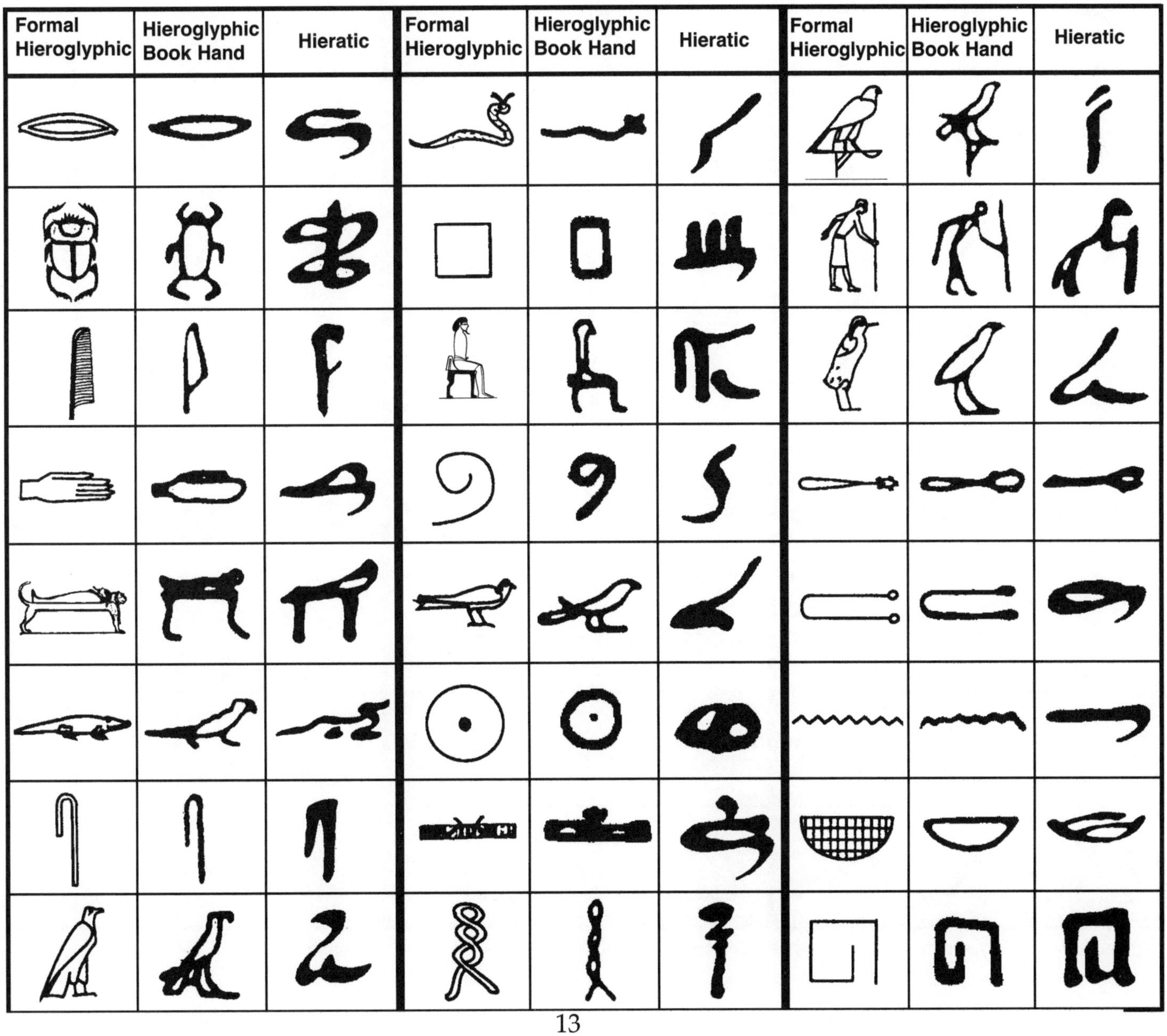

Formal Hieroglyphic	Hieroglyphic Book Hand	Hieratic	Formal Hieroglyphic	Hieroglyphic Book Hand	Hieratic	Formal Hieroglyphic	Hieroglyphic Book Hand	Hieratic

Formal Hieroglyphic	Hieroglyphic Book Hand	Hieratic	Formal Hieroglyphic	Hieroglyphic Book Hand	Hieratic	Formal Hieroglyphic	Hieroglyphic Book Hand	Hieratic

These Literary Hieratic of the Twelfth Dynasty (and the Formal Hieroglyphic and Hierogyphic Book Hand) are specimen transcriptions in a modern Egyptological hand. (See Gardiner, 10-D Plate II.)

THE ANTHON TRANSCRIPT

The "Anthon Transcript" is the name given to a single sheet of paper containing seven lines of characters transcribed by Joseph Smith Jr. from the gold plates from which the Book of Mormon was translated.

We are fortunate to have a record of figures from the gold plates, an even stronger external evidence of the Book of Mormon in light of Stan's translation. The Anthon Transcript exists; it is *tangible* evidence that the gold plates existed; the characters on it are the *actual* figures which Joseph Smith Jr. copied from the gold plates and left for examination. "The Anthon Transcript is also important to subsequent generations as an authentic sample of characters that were inscribed on the gold plates and thus one of the few tangible evidences of their existence." (*Encyclopedia of Mormonism*,Vol. 1, 44) The translation, as it should be, is a story directly from the Book of Mormon.

We were surprised at the vast amount of research done on the Anthon Transcript which substantiated the people involved, the language comparisons, and the fulfillment of prophecy.

Charles Anthon was a professor of classical studies at what is now Columbia University in New York from 1820 until his death in 1867. As an adjunct professor of languages and ancient geography, he was well known in 1828. Two letters written by Professor Anthon still exist confirming his visit with Martin Harris.

Joseph Smith tells the story of the Anthon Transcript in his own words:

Sometime in this month of February, the aforementioned Mr. Martin Harris came to our place, got the characters which I had drawn off the plates, and started with them to the city of New York. For what took place relative to him and the characters, I refer to his own account of the circumstances, as he related them to me after his return, which was as follows:

I went to the city of New York, and presented the characters which had been translated, with the translation thereof, to Professor Charles Anthon, a gentleman celebrated for his literary attainments. Professor Anthon stated that the translation was correct, more so than any he had before seen translated from the Egyptian. I then showed him those which were not yet translated, and he said that they were Egyptian, Chaldaic, Assyriac, and Arabic; and he said they were true characters. He gave me a certificate, certifying to the people of Palmyra that they were true characters, and that the translation of such of them as had been translated was also correct. I took the certificate and put it into my pocket, and was just leaving the house, when Mr. Anthon called me back, and asked me how the young man found out that there were gold plates in the place where he found them. I answered that an angel of God had revealed it unto him.

He then said to me, 'Let me see that certificate.' I accordingly took it out of my pocket and gave it to him, when he took it and tore it to pieces, saying that there was no such thing now as ministering of angels, and that if I would bring the plates to him he would translate them. I informed him that part of the plates were sealed, and that I was forbidden to bring them. He replied, 'I cannot read a sealed book.' I left him and went to Dr. Mitchell, who sanctioned what Professor Anthon had said respecting both the characters and the translation. (Joseph Smith History-1:63-65, Pearl of Great Price)

We would like to point out that Martin Harris took three things to Charles Anthon: (1) the characters which had been translated, (2) the translation of those characters, and (3) those characters "which were not yet translated." The Anthon Transcript we have appears to be the "characters which had been translated"—those Joseph "had drawn off the plates" and translated.

Why did Martin Harris take this transcript to the "learned" man in the first place? In one of a series of letters to W. W. Phelps, Oliver Cowdery says that the Angel Moroni told Joseph Smith, "The scripture [Isaiah 29:11-12] must be fulfilled before it is translated, which says that the words of a book which were sealed were presented to the learned, for this has God determined to leave man without excuse" (*Messenger and Advocate*, series of letters, 1834-1835, from Oliver Cowdery to W. W. Phelps). According to Stanley B. Kimball, Cowdery claimed that Joseph helped him in the preparation of these letters.

In more than one instance, Edward Stevenson, a member of the presidency of the First Quorum of the Seventy [1894] related, "It was manifested to the Prophet that a facsimile of characters must be copied and sent to the most learned professors of the country and that Martin Harris should be the bearer of them." (*Reminiscences of the Prophet Joseph* [Salt Lake City, 1893], 28-29) William Edwin Berrett claims

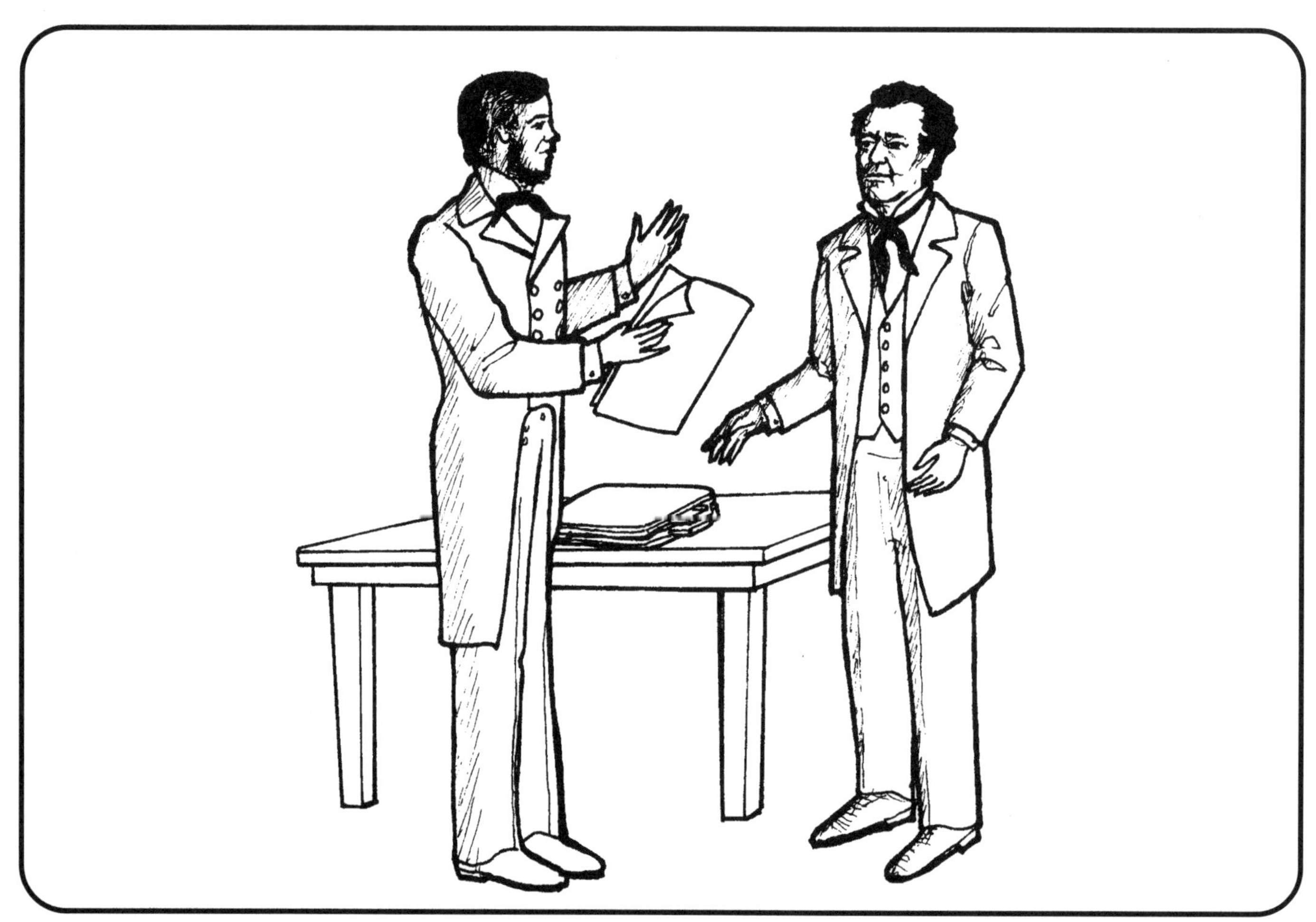

Martin Harris went to New York City and presented the characters which had been translated, with the translation thereof, to Professor Anthon.

that the prophecy was the primary factor which led Joseph to prepare the transcript of characters for Martin Harris to take to "learned men."

Joseph himself, in his 1832 account of the Harris-Anthon visit said:

> The Lord appeared to him [Harris] in a vision and shewed unto him his marvilous work which he was about to do and he imediately came to Su(s)quehanna and said the Lord had shown him that he must go to New York City with some of the c(h)aracters so we proceeded to coppy some of them and he took his Journy. (*The Papers of Joseph Smith* [Salt Lake City: Deseret Book, 1989], 1:9)

In reference to Joseph's preparation prior to translating the gold plates, Joseph's mother, Lucy Mack Smith, wrote:

> The first step that he was instructed to take in regard to this work was to make a facsimile of some of the characters, which were called reformed Egyptian, and to send them to some of the most learned men of this generation and ask them for a translation thereof. (*History of the Prophet*, 114)

This historical event fulfilled two prophecies! The first is from Isaiah, a Hebrew prophet and an adviser at the royal court in Jerusalem from approximately 740 to 701 B.C. The Bible Dictionary states: "Isaiah is the most quoted of all the prophets, being more frequently quoted by Jesus, Paul, Peter, and John (in his Revelation) than any other Old Testament prophet." Isaiah wrote:

> And the vision of all is become unto you as the words of a book that is sealed, which men deliver to one that is learned, saying, Read this, I pray thee: and he saith, I cannot; for it is sealed: And the book is delivered to him that is not learned, saying, Read this, I pray thee: and he saith, I am not learned. (Isaiah 29: 11-12)

The Inspired Version sheds even more light on this historical event, and suggests a motive for Charles Anthon's request for the book to be brought to him:

> And it shall come to pass, that the Lord God shall bring forth unto you the words of a book; and they shall be the words of them which have slumbered.
>
> And behold, the book shall be sealed; and in the book shall be a revelation from God, from the beginning of the world to the ending thereof . . . .
>
> But the book shall be delivered unto a man, and he shall deliver the words of the book, which are the words of those who have slumbered in the dust; and he shall deliver these words unto another, but the words that are sealed he shall not deliver, neither shall he deliver the book.
>
> For the book shall be sealed by the power of God . . . .
>
> But, behold, it shall come to pass, that the Lord God shall say unto him to whom he shall deliver the book, Take these words which are not sealed and deliver them to another, that he may show them unto the learned, saying, Read this, I pray thee.
>
> And the learned shall say, bring hither the book and I will read them; and now because of the glory of the world, and to get gain will they say this, and not for the glory of God. And the man shall say, I cannot bring the book for it is sealed. Then shall the learned say, I cannot read it.
>
> Wherefore it shall come to pass, that the Lord God will deliver again the book and the words thereof to him that is not learned; and the man that is not learned shall say, I am not learned. Then shall the Lord God say unto him, The Learned shall not read them, and I am able to do mine own work; wherefore thou shalt read the words which I shall give unto thee. (Inspired Version Isaiah 29:11-12, 20-22)

The second prophecy, written about 545 B.C., is from the Book of Mormon (2 Nephi 27:6-20):

> And it shall come to pass that the Lord God shall bring forth unto you the words of a book, and they shall be the words of them which have slumbered. And behold the book shall be sealed; and in the book shall be a revelation from God, from the beginning of the world to the ending thereof. Wherefore, because of the things which are sealed up, the things which are sealed shall not be delivered in the day of the wickedness and abominations of the people. Wherefore the book shall be kept from them. But the book shall be delivered unto a man [Joseph Smith], and he shall deliver the words of the book, which are the words of those who have slumbered in the dust, and he shall deliver these words unto another [Martin Harris]; but the words which are sealed [two-thirds of the gold plates] he shall not deliver, neither shall he deliver the book . . . . But behold, it shall come to pass that the Lord God shall say unto him [Joseph Smith] to whom he shall deliver the book: Take these words which are not sealed [the Anthon Transcript] and deliver them to another [Martin Harris], that he may show them unto the learned [Charles Anthon], saying: Read this I pray thee. And the learned [Charles Anthon] shall say: Bring hither the book, and I will read them. . . . And the man [Martin Harris] shall say: I cannot bring the book, for it is sealed. Then shall the learned [Charles Anthon] say: I cannot read it. Wherefore it shall come to pass, that the Lord God will deliver again the book and the words thereof to him that is not learned [Joseph Smith]; and the man that is not learned shall say: I am not learned. Then shall the Lord God say unto him: The learned shall not read them, for they have rejected them, and I am able to do mine own work; wherefore thou shalt read the words which I shall give unto thee.

Charles Anthon would be forever linked to the fulfillment of these prophecies by Latter-day Saints. Joseph Fielding Smith Jr. wrote:

> One of the most important predictions regarding the Book of Mormon is that found in the 29th chapter of Isaiah. . . . This prophecy was literally fulfilled when Martin Harris took copies of the engravings of the plates of the Book of Mormon to Professor Anthon in New York. . . . Mr. Anthon answered Martin in almost the language of Isaiah when he was informed that the book from which the characters were taken was sealed, said he: 'I cannot read a sealed book.' How remarkable it is that Isaiah said that the *words of the book* were delivered to one who was learned and that the *book* was delivered to the one who was not learned. How perfectly this harmonizes with the history of the case respecting Mr. Anthon and Joseph Smith! (*Doctrines of Salvation*, vol. 3 [Bookcraft: Salt Lake City, 1956], 2, emphasis added)

From the journal of George Q. Cannon, we have an account of his meeting with seventy-nine-year old David Whitmer, one of the three witnesses of the Book of Mormon. The meeting took place on February 27, 1884, in Richmond, Missouri. Brother Cannon relates:

> He had his son bring in the manuscript of the Book of Mormon, which he says is the only manuscript of which he knows anything. It is in the handwriting of several persons which he says were Oliver Cowdery, Emma Smith, Martin Harris . . . . This is the manuscript from which the printers, he says, set the type of the Book, and he pointed out to me where it had been cut for convenience as copy. . . . But with this was another paper which I thought of surpassing interest. It was the characters drawn by Joseph Smith himself for Martin Harris to show Professors Mitchell and Anthon. There were seven lines, the first four being about twice as long in size as the three last. Here was the very paper which Isiah [sic] saw in vision years before, and which he called the "words of a book." Though evidently long written, the characters were as clear and distinct as though just written. This

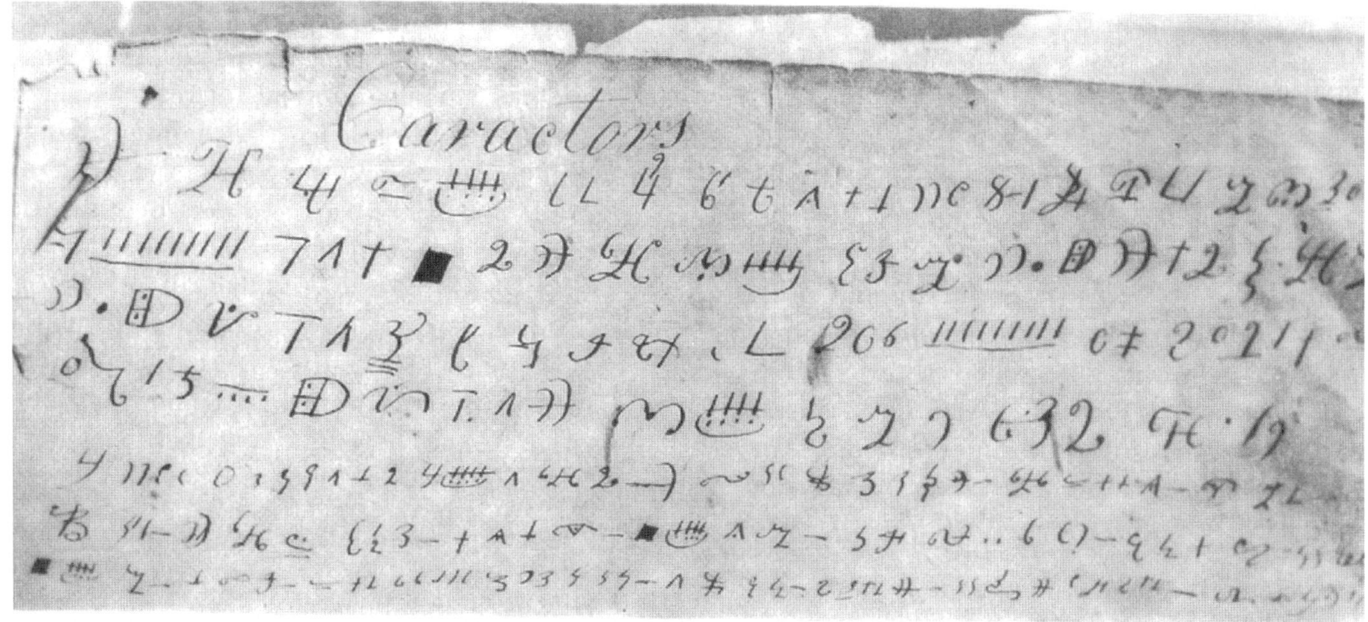
Caractors

Facsimile of the "Caractors" transcribed by Joseph Smith and taken to Charles Anthon by Martin Harris in 1828. This is the Anthon Transcript which Stan Johnson used for his translation. David Whitmer obtained this sheet along with the printer's manuscript of the Book of Mormon, from his brother-in-law, Oliver Cowdery, before Oliver died in 1850. Whitmer died on January 25, 1888, and the transcript passed on to his heirs. In April, 1903, the Whitmer heirs transferred the transcript to the Reorganized Church of Jesus Christ of Latter Day Saints. "Several copies of the Anthon transcript exist and have been published in various places. What appears to be the oldest version is in the possession of the Reorganized Church of Latter Day Saints at Independence, Missouri" ("Anthon Transcript Writing Found?" *Journal of Book of Mormon Studies*, F.A.R.M.S., Vol. 8, No.1, 1999, 68). See page 34 for an enlarged copy.

> also the case with the manuscript of The Book of Mormon. It was wonderfully well preserved and clear. This, David Whitmer and the family think (in which belief I share), is due to the power of God. (George Q. Cannon Journal, LDS Church Archives)

"The transcript is on a 'slip of paper eight inches long by three and one quarter inches wide.' It is written on paper much like that on which the manuscript of the Book of Mormon is written" (Ariel L. Crowley, "The Anthon Transcript," *The Improvement Era*, Jan. 1942, 15).

These descriptions of the Anthon Transcript certainly fit the transcript copy which Stan Johnson has translated. It is also the copy depicted in the *Encyclopedia of Mormonism*, under which is written:

> This document represents the Book of Mormon characters on the gold plates. It may be the transcript taken by Martin Harris to Charles Anthon in 1828, or a copy of it. The heirs of David Whitmer sold this document to the Reorganized Church of Jesus Christ of Latter Day Saints. This text is too short to be deciphered . . . . David Whitmer, who once owned the document, said it was this text that Martin Harris showed to Charles Anthon. . . . Even if the document is not the original, it almost certainly represents characters either copied from the plates in Joseph Smith's possession or copied from the document carried by Harris. (Courtesy Reorganized Church of Jesus Christ of Latter Day Saints, "The Auditorium" [Independence, Missouri, 1992]).

In a letter to Dr. John A. Widtsoe, Frederick M. Smith declared that the seven-line transcript headed by the word "Caractors" was with the handwritten manuscript of the Book of Mormon in the possession of David Whitmer in 1884.

David Whitmer died January 25, 1888, and the transcript was passed on to his heirs. In April, 1903, the Whitmer heirs transferred the transcript to the Reorganized Church of Jesus Christ of Latter Day Saints. A letter dated May 9, 1941, written to Apostle John A. Widtsoe, from Frederick M. Smith, president of the Reorganized Church reads:

> Dear Sir and Friend, . . . Without reasonable doubt we have the original paper taken by Martin Harris to Professor Anthon. In 1884, a committee of the Reorganized Church had a conference with David Whitmer. From July 8 to August 17 of that year this committee worked with Father Whitmer in comparing published Books of Mormon with the manuscript then in his possession. At this time this paper was with the manuscript, and it was exhibited by him to the committee and he stated it was the original taken to Professor Anthon. . . . The appearance of the fragment, eight inches by three and one-fourth inches, evidences its antiquity, and since 1924 we have kept it under glass. . . . With best wishes, I remain, Yours sincerely,
> Frederick M. Smith

We know of six copies of the transcript other than the one Stan used (although it would be no surprise to find others in existence, especially in light of modern technology). They all look very similar, having seven horizontal lines, the last three being significantly smaller than the first four. One is labeled: "Reproduction of a copy . . . by Sam Brannan." Another says it is "Traced in 1893 by Edward Stevenson [a member of the first Quorum of the Seventy in 1894] from the original copy." The third is a reproduction (1903) of the Stevenson copy. R. C. Webb made the fourth copy in 1915, though the original source for his copy is unknown. Two others appeared in *The Society for Early Historic Archaeology*: The Robert's photograph of 1930 (*A Comprehensive History of the Church of Jesus Christ of Latter-day Saints,* Salt Lake City: Deseret News Press, 1930, 1:106) and the Smith & Smith copy of 1908 (*History of the Church of Jesus Christ of Latter-day Saints,* Joseph Smith and Heman C. Smith, 1805-1835, vol. 1, no. 122, September, 1970).

A few reproductions are shorter than the seven lines and poorly copied, but still undoubtedly from the original Anthon Transcript. One day as I was doing research, I came upon a picture of a broadside (a sheet of paper, especially of a large size, printed on one side only and used in distribution or for posting) published in the book *My Kingdom Shall Roll Forth—Readings in Church History*, [The Church of Jesus Christ of Latter-day Saints, 1979].

I had used this book in teaching Gospel Doctrine classes and as a resource in teaching seminary, yet never before had page 6 meant so much to me! The broadside had three lines of the Anthon characters, which by now were very familiar to me. The exciting part was that the explanation over it said, "Gold-lettered on a black background, this broadside publicized the Book of Mormon in the 1830s." The 1830s! Joseph Smith was martyred on June 27, 1844, so this was actually used by the Church to publicize the Book of Mormon when Joseph was alive. Moreover, Joseph certainly would have refuted the characters had they not been at least similar to those he copied from the gold plates. Joseph also would have refuted the claims made on the broadside, which say it contains "A correct copy of the characters taken from the plates of the Book of Mormon!! Was translated from . . . the same that was taken to Professor Anthon of New York by Martin Harris."

The one known original copy is preserved in the LDS Church Historian's Office, Salt Lake City. On its reverse, along with the signature of Mrs. Hyrum Smith, is written: "This was formerly owned by Hyrum Smith. Sent to the

Gold-lettered on a black background, this broadside publicized the Book of Mormon in the 1830s

STICK OF JOSEPH,

TAKEN FROM THE

HAND OF EPHRAIM.

A CORRECT COPY

OF THE CHARACTERS TAKEN FROM THE PLATES THE

BOOK OF MORMON!!

Was translated from...the same that was taken to Professor Anthon of New York, by Martin Harris, in the year 1827 in fulfilment of Isaiah 29: 11, 12.

"The vision of all is become unto you as the words of a book that is sealed, which men deliver to one that is learned, saying, Read this I pray thee: and he saith; I cannot for it is sealed; And the Book is delivered to him that is not learned, saying, Read this, I pray thee, and he said, I am not learned."

"Truth shall spring out of the earth." –*Psalms 85–11.*

"I have written to Ephraim the great things of my law." –*Hosea 8–12.*

"Thus saith the Lord God, Behold I will take the Stick of Joseph, which is in the hand of Ephraim, and the tribes of Israel his fellows, and will put them with him, even with the stick of Judah, and make them one stick, and they shall be one in mine hand–*Ezekiel 37–19*

"Our fathers once had 'Sacred Book' like the white man have, but it was hid in the ground, since then Indian no more prevail against his enemies."–*An aged Indian of the Stockbridge tribe.*

Historian's Office, March 22, 1860, by his son, Joseph Fielding Smith."

We reproduced and enlarged the copy of the broadside using a magnifying glass, because it makes some interesting claims (see page 23). In addition to the aforementioned text, it states, "in fulfillment of Isaiah 29:11-12." It also quotes Ezekiel 37:19, suggesting that the Book of Mormon is the stick of Joseph. A quote from the aged Stockbridge Indian is on the bottom: "Our Fathers once had 'Sacred Book' like the white man have, but it was hid in the ground, since then Indian no more prevail against his enemies." This certainly concurs with the plight of the Lamanites in the Book of Mormon, since the gold plates were hid in the hill Cumorah by Moroni, around A.D. 420. Although the characters on this broadside are poorly copied, they are most certainly from the Anthon Transcript, as it claims they are. The one mistake on the sheet is the reference to the year 1827, instead of 1828, as the year Martin Harris took the transcript to Charles Anthon. Joseph copied some characters from December 1827 through February 1828, and possibly explains the discrepancy.

A similar copy appeared in 1884 in *The Prophet*, a paper published by the Church in New York and edited by Samuel Brannan, the presiding elder of a branch in New York City. Because the divergences from the original characters seem to be exactly like those in the broadside, and it makes the same claims as the broadside, it seems logical that it was copied from the broadside reproduced from *My Kingdom Shall Roll Forth.*

While Stan was immersed in the translation, I was having a wonderful time with the research on the project. I read and studied everything I could get my hands on concerning this event in Church history. Information began to almost fall at my feet. While I was standing in line at the BYU Bookstore during a seminary symposium, there on the rack in front of me were two wonderful research papers published by Foundation for Ancient Research & Mormon Studies, more commonly known as F.A.R.M.S. The titles jumped out at me. One was "Martin Harris' Visit with Charles Anthon—Collected Documents on the Anthon Transcript," another was "Shorthand Egyptian," by F.A.R.M.S. staff. In addition, I found "The Anthon Transcript: People, Primary Sources, and Problems," by Stanley B. Kimball. These were veritable gold mines of information with wonderful references to pursue. While teaching special education seminary in Utah County I had access to the libraries in several seminary buildings. Friends of ours who were aware of our project also began sending articles to us.

When James Reimschiissel, Stan's good friend, sent several articles on the Anthon Transcript, I learned quickly that I needed to be careful. One was from the July 1980 *Ensign* (69-73). At first, on seeing the source of the article, I thought it useful information, the title being "A Look At The Newly Discovered Joseph Smith Manuscript." However, James had written a warning "Watch out for Mark Hoffman Stuff!!!" across the top of the page and thereafter I did.

I was amazed to find so much information on this subject. Perhaps one of the most interesting facts I discovered was that Charles Anthon's credibility was in doubt. I had thought the story of the "sealed book prophecy," as referred to by Bruce R. McConkie in *Mormon Doctrine,* was familiar to most Latter-day Saints. After all, it is in our scriptures in the Pearl of Great Price, Joseph Smith—History, 1:63-65.

However, in February 1828, neither Charles Anthon nor anyone else, except Joseph Smith, could give an accurate translation of what was copied from the "gold plates." Ariel Crowley wrote:

> At the time of the Prophet only a handful of men in the whole world had any knowledge

of the Egyptian language beyond knowledge of its existence and the several forms which it had taken. The riddle of the Rosetta Stone was unsolved, the basis for its ultimate decipherment having been laid in 1822 in the French works of Champollion. (Ariel L. Crowley "The Anthon Transcript—An Evidence of the Truth of the Prophet's Account of the Origin of the Book of Mormon," *Improvement Era,* Jan. 1942, 60)

Jay M. Todd, in his book *The Saga of the Book of Abraham* (Salt Lake City: Deseret Book, 1969, 124), says that "Champollion's *Egyptian Grammar* did not appear in French until after Champollion's death in 1832, and it is the basis of American scholarship on translating Egyptian."

He concluded that the "good doctors could possibly attempt to decipher, but hardly translate" (Todd, 124). Todd was referring to Anthon and Mitchell's involvement with the Chandler papyri. The "Chandler papyri" were Egyptian papyri the Prophet purchased in 1835, from which he translated the writings of Abraham that are now published as part of one of the Church's standard works, The Pearl of Great Price. Certainly the same conclusion exists regarding the Anthon Transcript, for Chandler consulted them in 1833-35, six to eight years *after* Martin Harris took the transcript to Professor Anthon and Dr. Mitchell in 1828. If they were unable to read it in 1833-35, they certainly wouldn't have been able to read it six to eight years before. Todd, also wrote:

> The account and some rationale important to the understanding of the story perhaps have been best presented by William E. Berrett, administrator of the seminaries and institutes for the Church School System, and a well-founded Latter-day Saint historian and theologian.

He then quotes William E. Berrett, as follows:

> It is evident from various accounts and documents (Roberts, *Comprehensive History of the Church,* vol. I , chapter IX.) that Professors Anthon and Mitchell of New York viewed the two papers Harris had, one a transcript of characters without a translation and the other containing both characters and translation. . . . Neither Professor Anthon nor any other man could read the characters. Even at the date of this writing [1949] the language of the plates remains a hidden secret. Even had they been in close harmony with ordinary Egyptian hieroglyphics it is improbable that Professor Anthon could have read them, as that written language was then little known and no single American was as yet skilled in its reading. (Todd, 121-122)

While enrolled in a BYU Continuing Education class taught by Dr. Robert J. Matthews on the Pearl of Great Price, Stan and I learned about H. Donl Peterson's new book *The Story of the Book of Abraham* and purchased it as soon as it was available in 1995. I received further insight into many matters which helped me to better understand things pertaining to the early history of The Church of Jesus Christ of Latter-day Saints, as well as the science of Egyptology. Dr. Peterson passed away shortly after the manuscript was completed, and his book was published posthumously. He was the author of study guides and books on the Pearl of Great Price and the Book of Mormon, and was a professor of ancient scripture at BYU. He wrote:

> In 1822 the young French genius Jean Francois Champollion, with the aid of the trilingual Rosetta Stone, had first deciphered the ancient hieroglyphic writings in France, but his dictionary of Egyptian hieroglyphics would not be published in Europe until 1841. Hence, the American academicians whom Chandler consulted in 1833-35, were unable to read the papyrus records. At best, they could

only speculate on the meaning of some of the symbols when they could reach consensus on them.

We share the conclusion drawn by Stanley H. B. Kimball in his article "I Cannot Read a Sealed Book":

> . . . that Anthon and Mitchell recognized the characters as Egyptian, is, I believe, the most probable. In 1828 there were few if any in the United States who had sufficient knowledge of the Egyptian to have vouched for the correctness of Joseph Smith's translation. The basic books which led to an understanding of the Egyptian language, Champollion's *Grammaire 'egyptienne* and *Dictionnaire 'egyptienne,* appeared posthumously in 1836 and 1841. No serious work on the Egyptian language was done in the United States until the late nineteenth century. (*The Improvement Era*, February 1957, 104, 106)

Orson Pratt seemed to know of Anthon's limitations:

> Of course in the transcripts the professor [Anthon] would doubtless recognize some Egyptian characters of the hieratic Egyptian, and in the translation would also find a right interpretation of those characters . . . but beyond this I do not think he could give much confirmation as to the correctness of the translation" (B. H. Roberts, *Comprehensive History of the Church of Jesus Christ of Latter-day Saints*, vol. 1 [Salt Lake City: Desert News Press, 1930], footnote, 101-102).

We wholly agree with the opinion of Stanley H. B. Kimball, assistant professor of history, who wrote:

> We know that Martin Harris actually did consult with Charles Anthon, that Charles Anthon was acquainted with the latest discoveries pertaining to the Egyptian language, . . . However, this does not prove that Anthon knew Egyptian, only that he was familiar with its appearance and general structure. Champollion himself was just beginning to 'break' the language and could actually translate little more than royal titles . . . . not too much weight can be given the statement by Anthon that 'the translation was correct, more so than any he had before seen translated from the Egyptian,' except that he saw the similarity between the Book of Mormon characters and hieratic or demotic Egyptian. . . . *Even a reincarnated Egyptian could not have translated the 'Anthon Transcript,' because the 'reformed Egyptian' writing and language was such that 'none other people knoweth our language'* [Mormon 9:34]. (Stanley H. B. Kimball, "Charles Anthon and The Egyptian Language," *Improvement Era,* October 1960, 710,765, emphasis added)

Of interest to me is the fact that I had placed much weight on Charles Anthon's being a learned man in the sense of being able to translate the transcript correctly and thus *confirm* that Joseph had the correct translation. The account in Church history is Joseph's statement of what Martin Harris told him. Joseph did not substantiate Charles Anthon's ability to translate the characters. The real importance of the Anthon Transcript to the world lies in the fulfillment of the prophecy and the additional witness this provides to mankind in regard to the Book of Mormon being the word of God and the fact that Joseph translated it from the plates by the gift and power of God. Matthew 18:16 and 2 Nephi 27:14 say, "In the mouth of two or three witnesses every word may be established," and "In the mouth of as many witnesses as seemeth him good will he establish his word." In the article "The Anthon Transcript: People, Primary Sources, and Problems," Dr. Stanley B. Kimball wrote,

"Perhaps the real reason behind the event lies in an 'ecclesiastical imperative' that through sufficient witnesses to truth mankind will be left without excuse for having rejected God's word" (314).

We believe that the Anthon Transcript exists as a witness of the truthfulness of Joseph Smith's testimony of the facts surrounding the coming forth of the Book of Mormon from the plates of gold delivered by the angel Moroni and translated by the gift and power of God. Is it not interesting that all the "learned" people we've quoted in this book couldn't make a translation of these characters, yet an unlearned farm boy without the advantages of modern technology or educational resources translated the entire Book of Mormon in approximately sixty-three days? The F.A.R.M.S. staff paper "Martin Harris' Visit With Charles Anthon" explains, "Despite the inability to decipher the transcript, it should be borne in mind that the Rosetta Stone—despite its Greek parallels to the Demotic and Hieroglyphic text—took decades and tremendous efforts to decipher. . . . This important archeological artifact in Mormondom thus remains a mystery" (9). Further, "Although the only surviving Anthon Transcript may not be the original, has not been deciphered, and is too short for decoding, several Egyptologists have thought that it contains many readily recognizable Egyptian cursive characters" (7).

Many Egyptologists, as well as other linguists and the most knowledgeable scholars available, have verified that without a doubt the "Anthon" characters have a resemblance to certain Egyptian texts, yet they still cannot translate the Anthon Transcript. A great deal has been made over the fact that neither Charles Anthon nor any other American could read Egyptian at that time. *But* the Anthon Transcript is *not* pure Egyptian anyway. It had changed over the years into reformed Egyptian. It is recorded in the Book of Mormon:

> And now, behold, we have written this record according to our knowledge, in the characters which are called among us the reformed Egyptian, . . . But the Lord knoweth our language; and because that none other people knoweth our language, therefore he hath prepared means for the interpretation thereof. (Mormon 9:32, 34)

The Lord promised He would provide a way for the translation, and it was through the Prophet Joseph Smith, by means of the Urim and Thummim and by the gift and power of God, that he did it.

Stan simply studied Egyptian and several Native American languages in connection with research for his sculptures; and thus was, through this unique combination, able to make a literal translation of one short story in the Book of Mormon. The use of the Native American Languages along with the Egyptian seems to be the key to his success. This is the conclusion of James L. Barker, professor emeritus of modern languages, University of Utah, who wrote:

> If the testimony of Joseph Smith and the witnesses of the Book of Mormon is true, the Lamanites [Indians] continued undoubtedly to inherit the language which had been 'handed down and altered by us according to our manner of speech,' and they still speak it in modern forms. ("The Language of the Book of Mormon," *Improvement Era*, June 1960, 390)

It is these "modern forms" of Native American Indian languages combined with Egyptian which Stan used to make his translation.

We continue to be amazed that Stan translated the Anthon Transcript, but he did. We are grateful to be an instrument in some small way, in providing further testimony of the validity of Joseph Smith as a latter-day prophet. We testify that he was and is a prophet of God.

It was satisfying for us to read:

> If it can be shown that the characters on the transcript conform to ancient Egyptian characters [and Stan has—see Symbol References], another strong evidence for the divine inspiration behind the translation of the Book of Mormon will be added to the many such evidences already existing. . . . Should it be further shown that the characters on the transcript make connected thought [and Stan has shown that they do], the evidence for Joseph's inspiration will be more substantiated. (Crowley, "The Anthon Transcript," *The Improvement Era,* Jan. 1942, 60)

Joseph Smith is a prophet of God and was the instrument through which the kingdom of God and Christ's true church was restored to the earth in these latter days. He translated the Book of Mormon from the characters on the gold plates, by the gift and power of God so that we might have the fulness of the gospel in our day. We have taken these things to God, in prayer, and He has manifested the truth of these things to us by the power of the Holy Ghost which is the instrument through which we may know the truth of ALL things.

Stan's translation of this small portion of characters from the plates, known as the Anthon Transcript, is further testimony that the Book of Mormon came to us in the divine way Joseph said it did. The Native American Indians are truly the ancestors of the Book of Mormon Lamanite people. May we all read it and follow the principles taught therein on our safe journey back into our Father in Heaven's presence.

THE LANGUAGE DEVELOPMENT

The American Indians are the descendants of the Hebrew nation which came out of Jerusalem in 600 B.C. On the title page of the Book of Mormon, it says, "Wherefore, it is an abridgment of the record of the people of Nephi, and also of the Lamanites—Written to the Lamanites, who are a remnant of the house of Israel."

The four writing samples on the next page are all examples of reformed Egyptian.

The many branches of American Indian languages had a common root, which can be traced to ancient Hebrew and Egyptian.

The "tree" diagram on page 31, shows that the Native American languages can trace their roots to the Old World languages.

Reformed Egyptian

A cursive handwriting form.

The Anthon Transcript (known as the "Stevenson Copy"). *Improvement Era*, Jan. 1942, 58, 59

Micmac Hieroglyphics (The Lord's Prayer). (*Picture Writing of the American Indian*, Garrick Mallery, vol. II, 669.)

Literary Hieratic Egyptian of the Twelfth Dynasty, (Gardiner, 10, plate II).

Maori glyphs (*Maori Symbolism Report*, Ettie A. Rout [New York: Harcort, Brace & Co., Inc., 1926], 158).

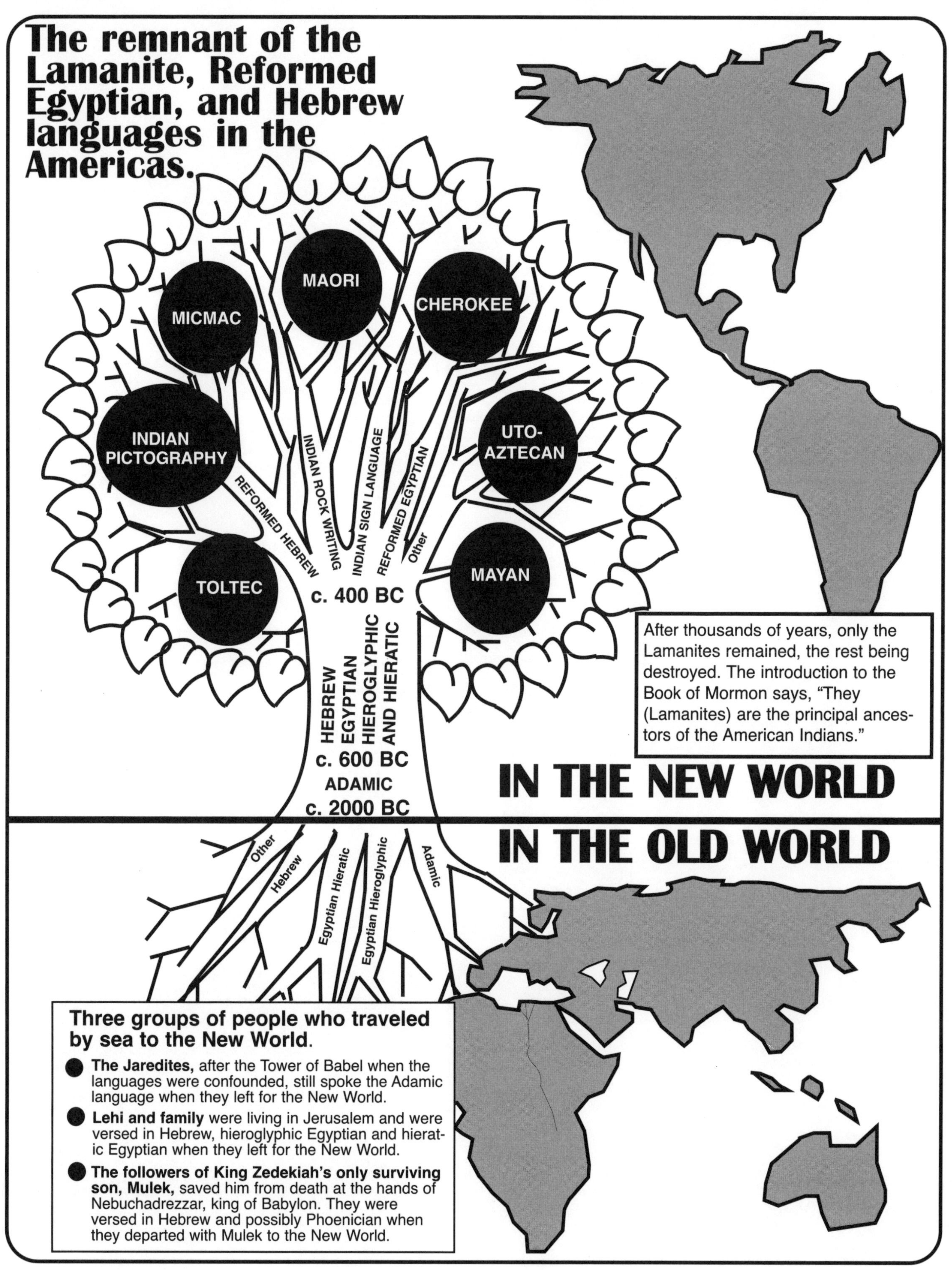

The remnant of the Lamanite, Reformed Egyptian, and Hebrew languages in the Americas.
MAORI
MICMAC
CHEROKEE
INDIAN PICTOGRAPHY
UTO-AZTECAN
TOLTEC
MAYAN
REFORMED HEBREW
INDIAN ROCK WRITING
INDIAN SIGN LANGUAGE
REFORMED EGYPTIAN
Other
c. 400 BC
HEBREW
EGYPTIAN
HIEROGLYPHIC
AND HIERATIC
c. 600 BC
ADAMIC
c. 2000 BC
After thousands of years, only the Lamanites remained, the rest being destroyed. The introduction to the Book of Mormon says, "They (Lamanites) are the principal ancestors of the American Indians."
IN THE NEW WORLD
IN THE OLD WORLD
Other
Hebrew
Egyptian Hieratic
Egyptian Hieroglyphic
Adamic
Three groups of people who traveled by sea to the New World.
The Jaredites, after the Tower of Babel when the languages were confounded, still spoke the Adamic language when they left for the New World.
Lehi and family were living in Jerusalem and were versed in Hebrew, hieroglyphic Egyptian and hieratic Egyptian when they left for the New World.
The followers of King Zedekiah's only surviving son, Mulek, saved him from death at the hands of Nebuchadrezzar, king of Babylon. They were versed in Hebrew and possibly Phoenician when they departed with Mulek to the New World.

THE TRANSLATION

As Stan enlarged the characters on the Anthon Transcript using a magnifying glass and his well-trained artist's eye, he immediately recognized several of the signs. His years of Egyptian and Native American language study combined with a cryptanalysis-type approach provided him with the key which unlocked the Anthon Transcript. Untold hours of hard work, break-throughs in unfamiliar languages, and spiritual promptings still lay ahead.

Stan has a passion for studying Egyptian and Native American languages. He had compiled over 20, three-inch binders bulging with Egyptian and Native American signs and their meanings, which were the backbone of his translation process. He had found over 200 signs in Egyptian and Native American, which were identical, leading him to the conclusion that they had a common source. He also used his extensive research library which includes books on Egyptian and Native American customs, legends, translations, art, and history, as well as two Egyptian encyclopedias, to decipher and document his translation.

Stan started the actual translation by randomly writing down the meanings of signs with which he was familiar above the Anthon characters. He was so excited! He knew many signs and could document them with *at least* two other signs that were similar or exactly the same. Time after time he would say, "Polly, come look at this, I know what it means! I *really* know what it means!"

Quite early in his translation process, the story was familiar to us, yet Stan refused to look at the Book of Mormon text. It was still incredulous to us that he really could translate the Anthon Transcript, and he was afraid that it might compromise his work.

Some of the signs remained a mystery to Stan as he labored over them for untold hours. He often stayed up until 1 a.m. and got up a 5 a.m. He was supporting his family with the sculpting and art business, and put in long days at the studio and foundry in addition to his work on the Anthon Transcript.

He felt that he was receiving help beyond his own abilities as he worked on the translation. One day a handsome Maori walked right into our studio and handed Stan what turned out to be a Rosetta Stone. He then walked out and was never seen again. It was a story written in Maori (along with the English translation) of the Maori trek from Egypt to the Americas to New Zealand (see p. 103). This opened the door to the understanding of several previously untranslated symbols. Once he was awakened in the early morning hours, being told in his mind that if he didn't get up right then and work on his translation, he would lose something very important. He arose, sat down at his desk, and began to work on some symbols which he suspected could be the "And it came to pass" sign. All of a sudden, it became crystal clear to him. At first, it seemed too good to be true. He counted the number of "And it came to pass" phrases in the Ether text, and the number of occurances in the transcript, and they were both seven. It matched perfectly! It was an Egyptian hieratic symbol incorporation (see Symbol Reference section, p. 74).

Stan really does know what the Anthon Transcript means! Graciously, he's made heroic efforts to help us all understand the hows and whys of his translation through exhaustive and thorough documentation. He shows his *literal* translation one symbol at a time, while coordinating it with the story of Joseph Smith translated by the gift and power of God. The Symbol Reference section of this book demonstrates the superfluous effort Stan has made to substantiate every symbol, hopefully satisfying both the curious and the critical.

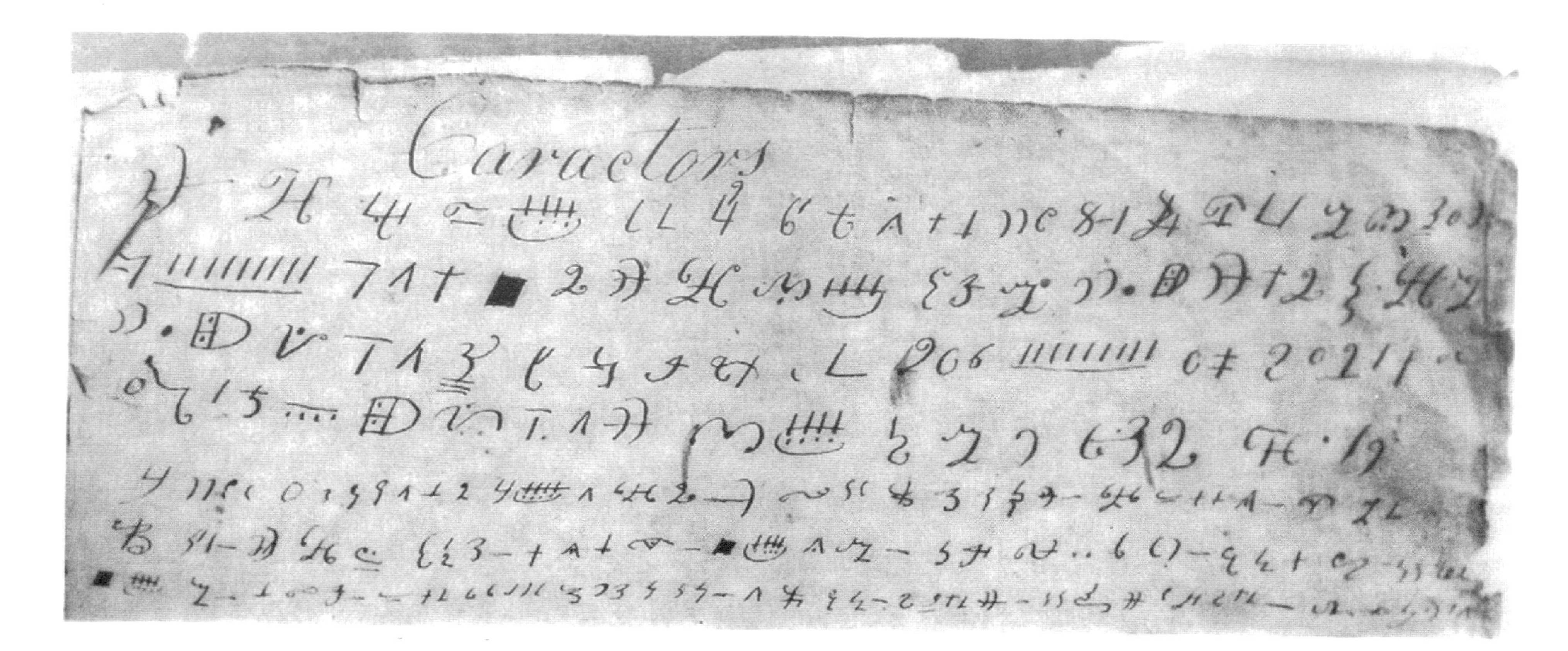

Facsimile of the "Caractors" transcribed by Joseph Smith and taken to Charles Anthon by Martin Harris in 1828.

This is the Anthon Transcript which Stan used for his translation. David Whitmer obtained this sheet along with the printer's manuscript of the Book of Mormon, from his brother-in-law, Oliver Cowdery, before Oliver died in 1850. Whitmer died on January 25, 1888, and the transcript passed on to his heirs. In April, 1903, the Whitmer heirs transferred the transcript to the Reorganized Church of Jesus Christ of Latter Day Saints. "Several copies of the Anthon transcript exist and have been published in various places. What appears to be the oldest version is in the possession of the Reorganized Church of Latter Day Saints at Independence, Missouri" ("Anthon Transcript Writing Found?" *Journal of Book of Mormon Studies*, F.A.R.M.S., Vol. 8, No.1, 1999, 68).

The following page shows Stan's enlarged reproduction of the original copy of the Anthon Transcript and his translation.

Starting on page 36, is Stan's translation of the Anthon Transcript. These seven horizontal lines were copied from the gold plates by Joseph Smith. The 213 "caractors" [sic] read right to left. Stan has enlarged each of the 213 symbols and shown (in the notes on the bottom of the pages) a simple translation. The Ether text is shown for comparison, at the top of each page. The small "SR" beneath each translation, refers to the Symbol Reference (in the Appendix, p. 70), where each "caractor" is documented and compared, in great detail, with well established signs and symbols.

The Anthon Transcript (Read right to left):

Copy and Translation by Stan Johnson, July 5, 1994, ©After reproduction of Original copy in the "Improvement Era" January 1942.

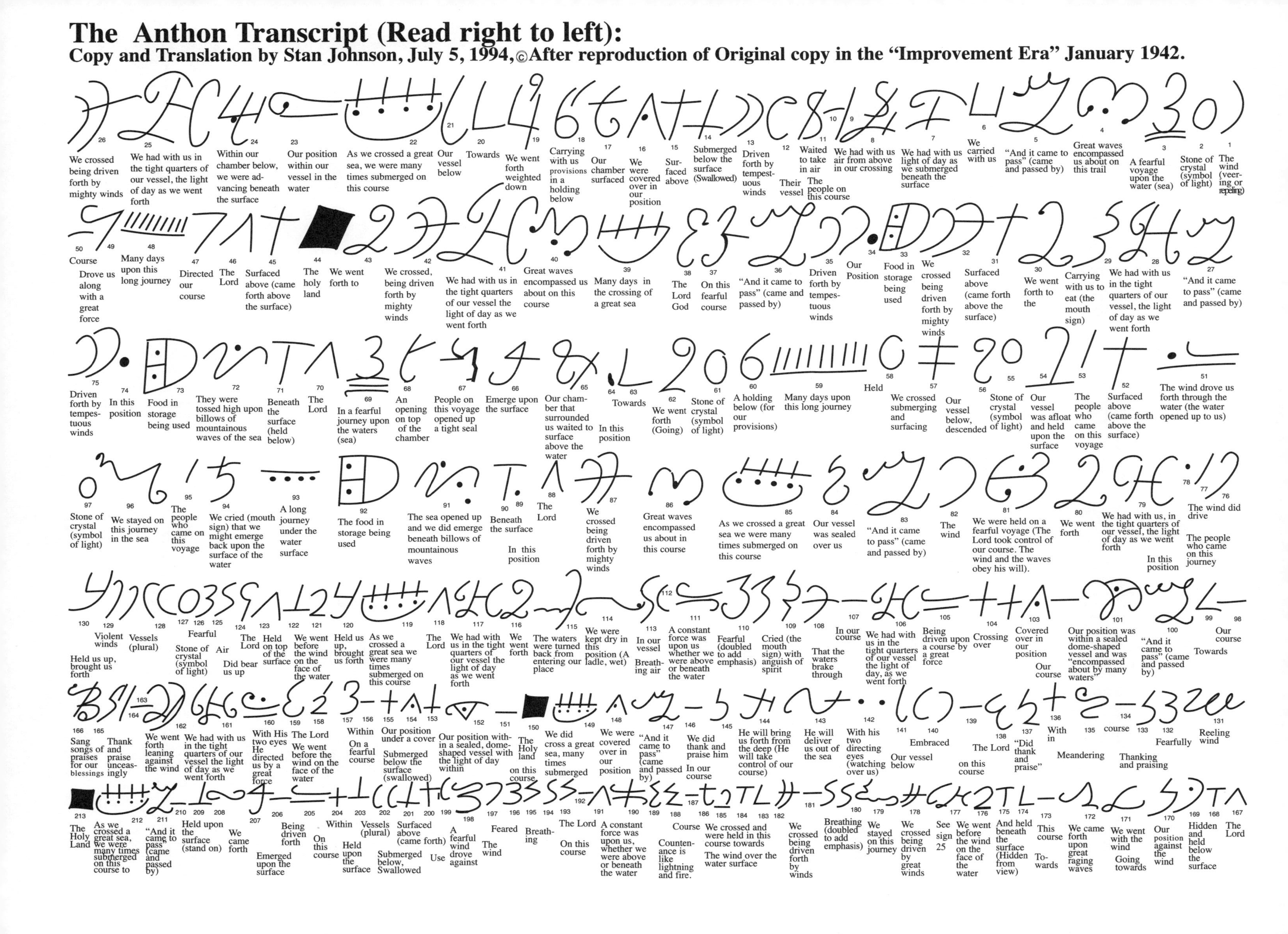

ETHER, CHAPTER 6.

THE STORY OF THE JAREDITES CONTINUED—THEIR VESSELS LIGHTED BY MIRACLE—THROUGH THE DEPTHS OF THE SEA TO THE PROMISED LAND

1. And now I, Moroni, proceed to give the record of Jared and his brother. (See also Ether 2:16-25)

2. For it came to pass after the Lord had prepared the stones which the brother of Jared had carried up into the mount, the brother of Jared came down out of the mount, and he did put forth the stones into the vessels which were prepared, one in each end thereof; and behold, they did give light unto the vessels.

Start (This is were the Anthon text begins.)

3. And thus the Lord caused stones (2) to shine in darkness, to give light (2), (7) unto men, women, and children (9), that they might not cross (4) the great waters (3), (22), (4) in darkness (16).

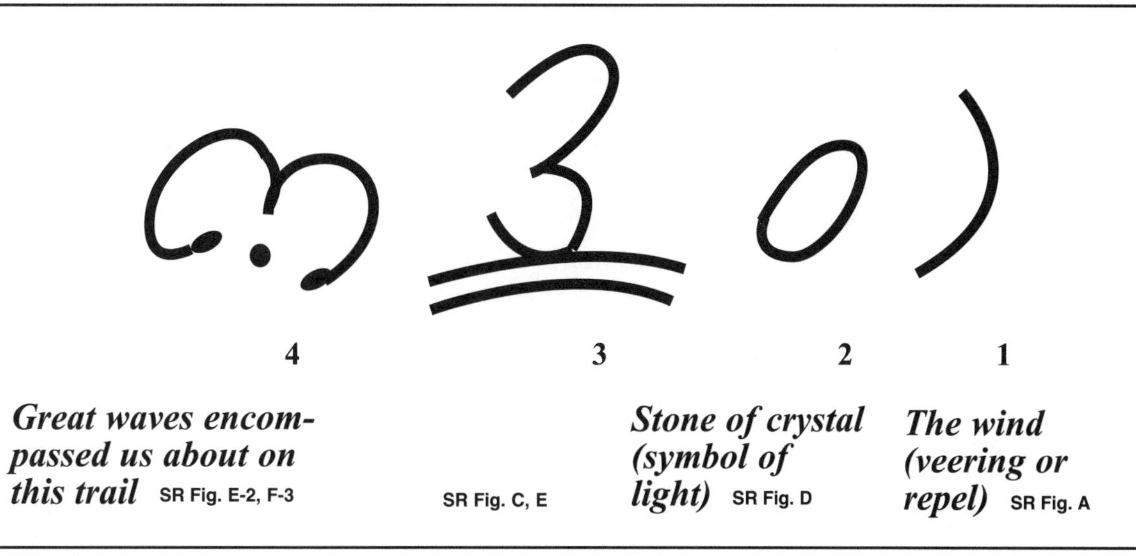

This reformed Egyptian text reads from right to the left. **The first symbol** in the text is the Indian "veering" or "repel" sign and in this situation relates to wind (*The Rocks Begin To Speak,* LaVan Martineau, p. 160, chart 8 [22]), and denotes a bad place to be (see symbol number 82). **The second sign** is the Indian symbol for light. It is in the form of a crystal stone. In the Navajo ceremonial "the crystals are symbolic of light, fire, and truth and are said ceremonially to light prayer sticks." In many legend they provide both illumination and fire (Tom Bahti, *Southwestern Indian Ceremonials* [Las Vegas: KC Publications, 1970], 8). **The third sign** is a Micmac symbol for fear . It is seated upon the Indian and Egyptian symbol for "wate to indicate a fearful course on the sea. **Sign number 4** is the symbol of a great encompassing movement over three dots. Three dots in a row (a broken line like this is the Indian sign for footsteps or a path — a weak or fragile trail off the beaten path) encompassed about by a raging, storm-tossed sea (Garrick Mallery, *Picture-Writing of the American Indians* [New York: Dover Publications, 1972] p. 716, fig. 1183).

Note: For more information about these signs, see the Symbol Reference (SR).

4. And it came to pass (5) that when they had prepared (6) all manner of food (18), (33), (73), (92)...

13	12	11	10	9	8	7	6	5
Driven forth by tempestuous winds SR Fig. A-3	***Their vessel*** SR Fig. B	***Waited to take in air*** SR Fig. P, H-2	***The people on this course*** SR Fig. H, K		***We had with us air from above in our crossing*** SR Fig. P, G-8, H-4	***We had with us light of day as we submerged beneath the surface*** SR Fig. H-4, 7	***We carried with us*** SR Fig. H-1, 10	***And it came to pass" (came and passed by)*** SR Fig. G

The **Fifth Symbol** in the text is identical to the Egyptian hieratic sign and is a symbol incorporation combining legs and the dual symbol and depicts the idea to come and pass by, seek, travel. This sign appears seven times in the Anthon text (see symbol numbers 27, 36, 83, 100, 149, 213) and seems to be related to the phrase "and it came to pass" which also appears seven times in Ether 6:3-13. (Sir Alan Gardiner, *Egyptian Grammar* [Oxford: Griffth Institute Ashmolean Museum, 1976], p. 457, D (54), 536 Z(4), 556 (\\), 532, X4 (6) 582 (hhy). **Symbol 6** is an Indian sign incorporation with the "towards" sign and the sacred Micmac sign for "the people who came on this voyage" . They are connected to depict the idea "to carry" or to hold up. **Symbol 7** is a common Indian gesture for day . It is when the index and thumb form a circle (remaining fingers closed) and are passed from east to west" (Mallery, vol. II, p. 698 fig. 1132). The vertical line is the man sign and is passing down through a horizontal line depicting an Indian and Egyptian sign for submergence, swallowed (Gardiner, page 462, F-10) or crossing below the water surface, and is also shown having the light of day as it went beneath the surface. The **Symbol Incorporation 8** has the Egyptian hieratic sign for "legs walking" and when combined with other signs, it denotes "movement" or "going toward," "come" (Mallery, vol. I, p. 457, D(54). The Moqui indian sign is a symbol for "breath" (Mallery, vol. II, p. 705). Note that the "leg" sign is carrying the "breath" symbol. At the end of the leg sign is another "submerged" symbol to denote that they went beneath the surface having with them air to breath. **Symbol 9** is the "man" sign and represents the people who came on this journey. **Symbol 10** is the "path" or "course" that they were on. **Symbol 11** is a repeat of the Moqui "breath" symbol. This "S" symbol in Hittite is "breath," "wind," or "spirit," (Mallery, vol. II, p. 663). The Indian sign for "to wait" is a slanting vertical line. The people had to wait to surface to take in air into their vessel (**Symbol 12**) a "repel" or "veering" sign in Indian (*The Rocks Begin To Speak,* Martineau, p. 125, fig. 64, symbol 6)*, or "end" sign in Egyptian (see E.A. Wallis Budge, Egyptian Book of the Dead* [New York: Dover Publications, 1967] p. 703, 633). **Symbol 13** is like symbol number 1, a veering or end sign, and is doubled to add emphasis and can denote a veering force like wind (see symbol numbers 129 and 169).

(Verse 4 cont.) ...that thereby they might subsist (18), (19), (29), (110) upon the water (3), (22), (51), (69), (85), (106), (107), (113), (152), (163) and also food (33), (73), (92) for their flocks (29), (110) and herds, and whatsoever beast or animal or fowl that they should carry (19) with them—...

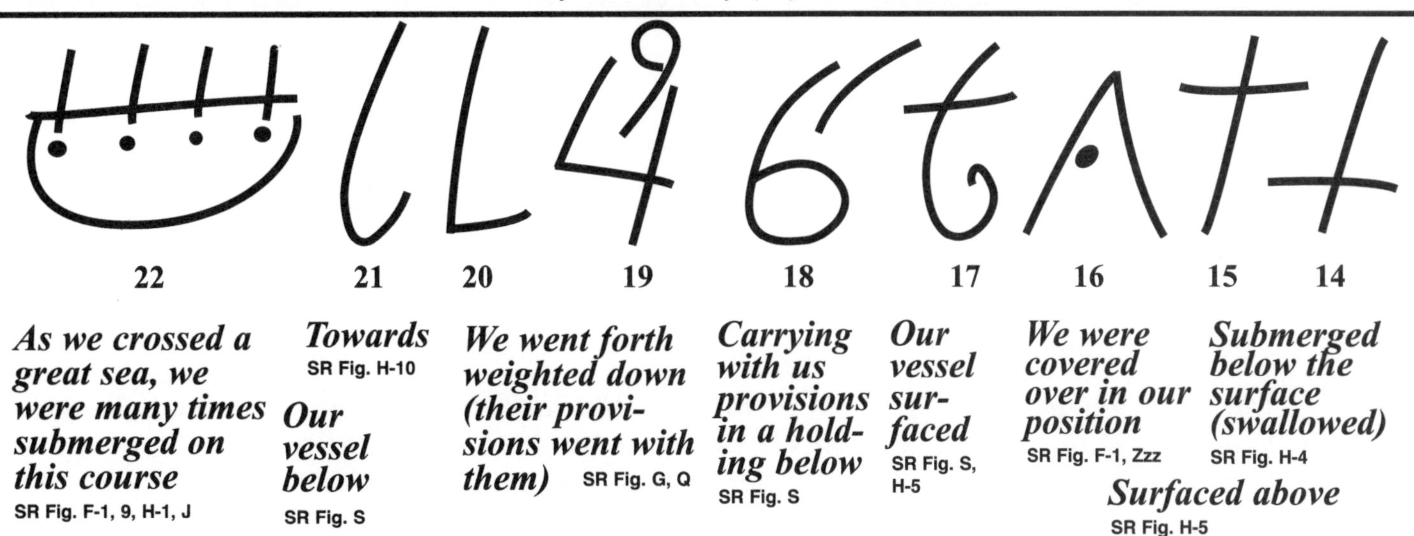

The **fourteenth and fifteenth symbols** depict the idea that the people on this voyage went below thesurface of the water and then surfaced again (much as a submarine would do). **Symbol 14** is an Indian and Egyptian sign for swallow, submerge or below (Gardiner, p. 462, F-10). **Symbol 16** indicates that the people's position who came on this journey were under a cover that would conceal them in darkness if they couldn't produce an artificial light. The Indian sign for covered, closed or hidden is a "V" turned over ∧ . A turned-over "V" can indicate "dark" or "closed" with a dot (a position sign) underneath (see Martineau, p. 152). They were in a closed vessel that had the capability of going beneath the water surface. They had their own light source in the form of light crystals in their vessel (Symbol 2). **Symbol 17** is the sign for a vessel that is deep beneath the surface and is coming forth or surfacing. **Symbol 18** is the sign for "provisions" in a holding below They went weighted down **(Symbol 19).** This sign is similar to Symbol 6. The "man sign" | with the "holding " sign being supported on top of the "man sign" to say that their provisions went with them. **Symbol 20** is specifically a Micmac Indian sign (and also some other tribes). It is the sign for "going towards," "not turning aside," or "am going" (Mallery, vol. II, p. 669; Martineau, p. 159, 160). The vertical line | is the sign of man, the voyagers. The horizontal line — at the base of the vertical line indicates travel. **Symbol 21** is the sign of a path or ladder descending down to a chamber (the symbol for cliff dwelling is a path or ladder descending beneath a horizon sign and leads down to a cliff dwelling or chamber sign (Martineau, p. 27, 28). In **Symbol 22** we learn that the voyagers were crossing a great sea , and were many days ("sequence, |||||| "number" or "count," "tally") (Mallery, p. 172; Martineau, p. 113, fig. 57(K), 131, 138, 13) in this crossing and were submerged .in this sea a great part of the time on this course (Mallery, vol. II, p. 480, fig. 668).

(Verse 4 cont.) ...**and it came to pass** (27) that when they had done all these things, they got aboard (25), (28) of their vessels or barges (12), (17), (18), (24), (25),...

30	29	28	27	26	25	24	23
We went forth to the SR Fig. G-8	***Carrying with us to eat provisions (the mouth sign)*** SR Fig. Y	***We had with us in the tight quarters of our vessel, the light of day as we went forth*** SR Fig. B, H-7, K-1	***And it came to pass (came and passed by)*** SR Fig. G	***In this crossing, we were driven forth by mighty winds*** SR Fig. F-5	***We had with us in the tight quarters of our vessel, the light of day as we went forth*** SR Fig. B, H-7, K-1	***Within our chamber below, we were advancing beneath the surface*** SR Fig. F. Q, S	***Our position within the water in our vessel*** SR Fig. E, F

Symbol 23 is the Egyptian sign to depict water (the position sign for the people who came on this voyage is shown encompassed under the water surface (Martineau, p. 28, 110 fig. 55-a 114, fig. 59-6-c, 160). **Symbol 24** is an incorporation of six signs, all of which have been described. The sign for the "path" or "course" together with the sign for "man" is the sign for "going towards" . The "position" sign below the "path sign" means "under cover" or "beneath the surface." The "man" sign together with the "towards" sign are the symbols for "we carried with us." When we add to this incorporation the "chamber below sign" (the "ladder" and "chamber"), we have the meaning that the people on this course in their chamber were advancing along beneath the water surface. **Symbol 25** is an incorporation of five signs. The Symbol for "day" (see Symbol 7) is joined to the Egyptian "leg" sign (see Symbol 5) to depict that the people had with them a light (a stone crystal) in their "chamber" (see Symbol 12) as they "went forth" on their "course" . **Symbol 26** is an incorporation of four signs. The "veering" or "end" sign that we saw in symbol 13 is doubled to add emphasis and may again denote wind or the water current. The sign for a "course" or "path" is stretched across them to depict the idea that they "crossed" the sea (see Symbol 22) on The water currents and were driven forth by wind. **Symbol 27** is a repeat of the sign "and it came to pass" (see Symbol 5). **Symbol 28** is is a repeat of the sign "We had with us in the tight quarters of our vessel, the light of day as we went forth (see Symbol 26). **Symbol 29** is the Maori "mouth" sign. On top of the mouth is the same sign to depict the "provisions" they had with them (see Symbol 18). **Symbol 30** is the sign that we described in Symbol 19. It is the Egyptian leg sign for "we went forth to" (see also Symbol 5).

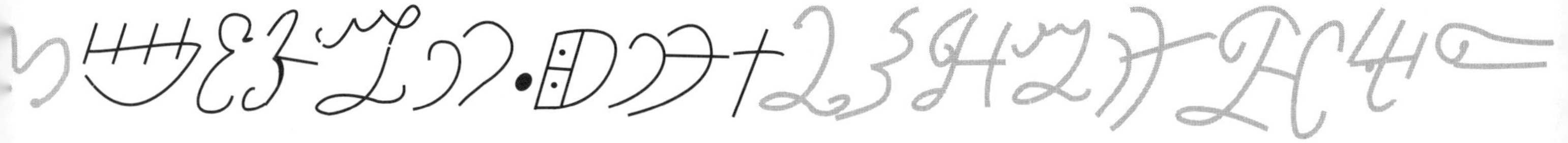

(Verse 4 cont.) ...and set forth (26) into the sea (22), (39), commending themselves (37) unto the Lord (38), (81) their God.

39	38	37	36	35	34	33	32	31
Many days in crossing a great sea	***The Lord God***	***On this fearful course***	***And it came to pass. (came and passed by)***	***Driven forth by tempes-tuous winds***	***Our position***	***Food in storage being used***	***In this crossing, we were driven forth by mighty winds***	***Surfaced above (came forth above the surface)***
SR Fig. H-4, K-1, J	SR Fig. X	SR Fig. C, K	SR Fig. G	SR Fig. A-3	SR Fig. F-1	SR Fig. Z, I-4	SR Fig. A-4, 5	SR Fig. H-5

Symbol 31 is the same sign as Symbol 15 and denotes that they "came forth." **Symbol 32** is a repeat of the symbol 26. **Symbol 33** is the sign for the food they ate on this journey. It is very simular to a Maya Indian glyph for "food"  (Martineau, p. 144, fig. 77c). The Two rectangle shapes on the left side of the sign are symbolic of "place." The dot within the box is the "position" sign and indicates "something there" and depicts the food in storage. The square corners on the sides of the rectangles are the symbol for a "man-made" place (the storage place in the Chamber). The rounded symbol attached to the right side of the sign is a "bowl"  turned on its side and is the Indian sign for food being used or spilled (Martineau, p. 160). **Symbol 34** is a position sign and is large and blackened to depict a bad position. **Symbol 35** is the same sign as described in symbol 13. **Symbol 36** is a repeat of the symbol 5 and 27. **Symbol 37** is the Micmac sign for fear (Mallery, Vol. 2, p. 668, fig. 1082.) The horizontal line attached to the sign is the symbol for course. It is connected to the sign "fearful" to signify that the people on this journey got aboard of their "vessels" (or "barges") and set forth on this fearful journey upon the sea, "commending themselves unto the Lord their God" (Ether 6:4). **Symbol 38** is the Micmac and Maori Indian sign for "Lord." **Symbol 39** is a modified Symbol 22 and appears without the four dots, depicting the submerged course in the water.

5. And it came to pass (76) that the Lord God (38) caused that there should be a furious wind (42) blow upon the face (185), of the waters (40) towards (43) the promised land (44);...

47	46	45	44	43	42	41	40
Directed our course	***The Lord***	***Surfaced above***	***The holy land***	***We went forth towards***	***In this crossing, we were driven forth by furious winds***	***We had with us in the tight quarters of our vessel, the light of day as we went forth***	***Great waves encompassed us about on this course***
SR Fig. K-7	SR Fig. R	SR Fig. H-5	SR Fig. Zz	SR Fig. G-8	SR Fig. A-5	SR Fig. B, K, G-8, H-7	SR Fig. F-3

Symbol 40 is a repeat of the Symbol 4. **Symbol 41** is a repeat of the Symbol 25. **Symbol 42** is a repeat of the Symbol 2. **Symbol 43** is a repeat of the Symbol 30 with only one change**.** There is a descending sign on the top (see Symbol 62). **Symbol 44** is a square the Indian sign for a place or settlement. The square is said to represent the Hopi village of Oraibi (Martineau, p. 160 chart 8, Symbol 21). The "square corners" is the symbol for man-made. The rectangular enclosure is the Egyptian sign for castle, mansion, temple, tomb, or house place. When the "place" sign is filled in solid it indicates in Indian that there is something there holy (sacred), strong, bad or encumbered and other related meanings. To identify the specific meaning, you must see how the sign appears in context with other related signs that appear with it. **Symbol 45** is a repeat of the symbol number 15, **Symbol 46** could be the Indian sign for a "tepee" and is another way to say "Lord" in Micmac (Mallery, Vol. II, p. 669, fig. 1083). The Egyptian sign for "pyramid" can also be the symbol of "Lord" or "God." The Hittite sign for "Lord" , is identical to symbol 46 (Mallery, Vol. II, p. 663, fig. 1083). **Symbol 47** is the "man" sign holding up the sign for "course" (see Symbol 9 and 10), possibly to depict "directing this journey."

(Verse 5 cont.) ...and thus they were tossed upon the waves (72) of the sea (39) before the wind (32), (35), (42), (51), (75), (76).

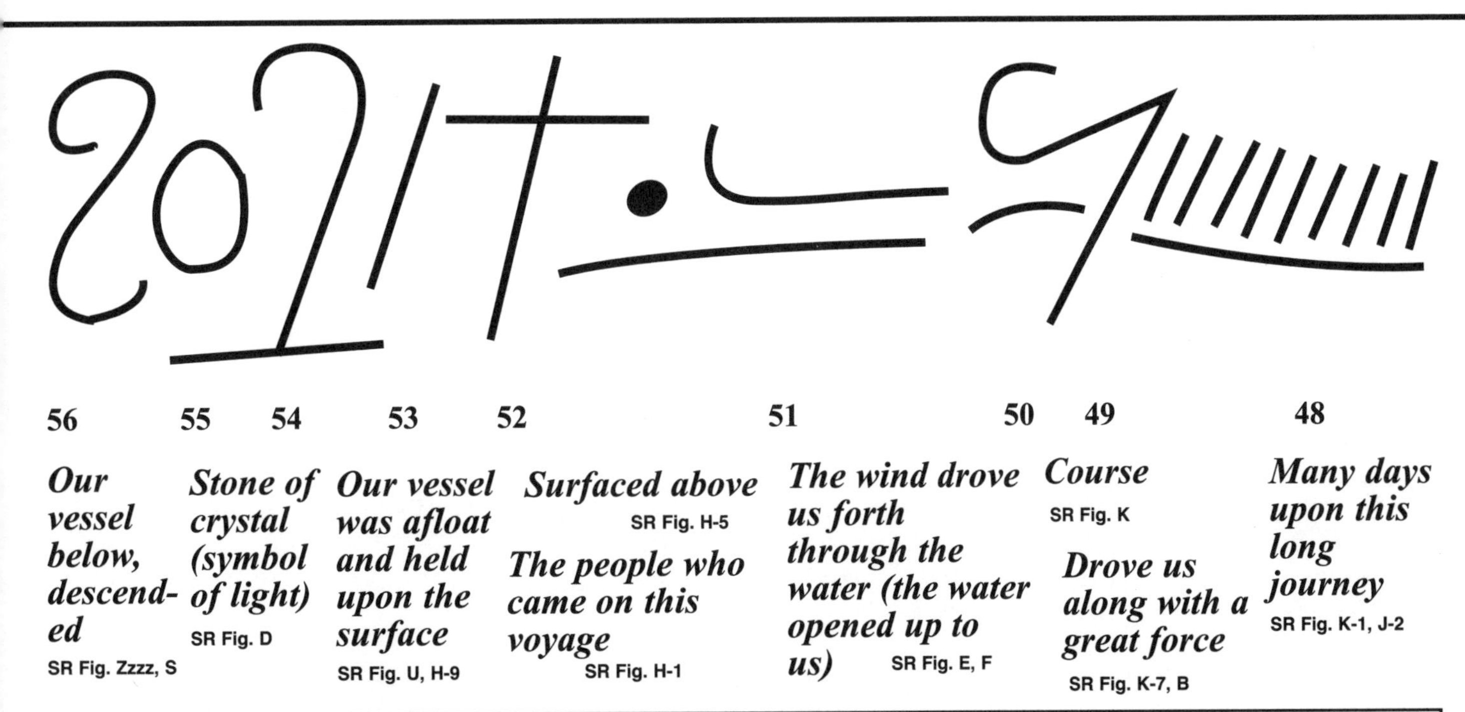

Symbol 48 is the Indian "sequence" sign that depicts many, a number or count, or tally (Martineau, p. 131, fig. 57-K, 138, 172). The sign under the sequence symbol is a line that depicts a long journey. **Symbol 49** is a repeat of Symbol 47 with one addition. The "wind" sign is added to the end of the "trail" Symbol to denote that the wind drove upon this course. **Symbol 50** is a repeat of Symbol 10. **Symbol 51** is a repeat of the sign of water that we saw in Symbol 3. The position sign is seen in great turbulence and being driven forth "by the fierceness of the wind." **Symbol 52** is a repeat of Symbol 15. **Symbol 53** is a repeat of Symbol 9. **Symbol 54** is the Navajo sign for afloat. It is the "holding" sign above the surface with the vessel or a "hidden" . sign attached on top (Martineau, p. 103 [3], [30], p. 28, chart 3, and p. 101, fig. 49, symbol 35). This arch- shaped sign on top resembles a shepherd's crook and is the sign for the dome-shape ceiling of the chamber. **Symbol 55** is a repeat of Symbol 55. **Symbol 56** may be the "deep-down chamber" sign that we saw in Symbol 17 with the descending sign on top (see Symbol 62).

6. And it came to pass (83) that they were many times (22), (48), (39), (59) buried (4), (14), (22), (23), (24), (39), (40), (57), (86), (91) in the depths (14), (22), (23), (25), (39), (91), of the sea (22), (39), (85) because of the mountain waves (4), (23), (40), (72), (86), (91), (146) which broke upon them (4), (23), (40), (51), (86), (91),...

64	63	62	61	60	59	58	57
This position SR Fig. F-1	***Towards*** SR Fig. H-10,	***Went forth (going)*** SR Fig. H-10, Zzzz	***Stone of crystal (symbol of light)*** SR Fig. D	***A holding below (for our provisions)*** SR Fig. S, I-6	***Many days upon this long journey*** SR Fig. K-1, J-2	***Held*** SR Fig. I-6	***We crossed submerged and on the surface*** SR Fig. K-5,

Symbol 57 is the Indian sign to "cross over." It is unusual to see this sign rendered in a vertical position. When rendered this way, the sign has the same meaning as Symbol 14 and 15 in this text ┼, ┼. **Symbol 58** is a difficult sign to decipher. I couldn't be sure if it was the sign for "stone," "chamber," or "holding." It might even be a sign indicating how many days the people were upon the water. **Symbol 59** is the same sign as Symbol 48. **Symbol 60** is the same sign as Symbol 18. **Symbol 61** is the same sign as Symbol 2. **Symbol 62** is another difficult sign for me to identify. The Symbol looks as if it could be similar to Symbol 43 or it could be a new sign incorporation. The spiral at the top of the sign is the Indian sign for descending (Martineau, p. 18, 19, fig. 10-c, d). The bottom portion of the sign resembles **Symbol 63** which is the "towards" sign and is the same sign as Symbol 20. **Symbol 64** is the same sign as Symbol 34.

(Ether 2:20) And the Lord said unto the brother of Jared: Behold, thou shalt make a hole in the top, and also in the bottom; and when thou shalt suffer for air thou shalt unstop the hole and receive air. And if it be so that the water come in upon thee, behold, ye shall stop the hole, that ye may not perish in the flood....

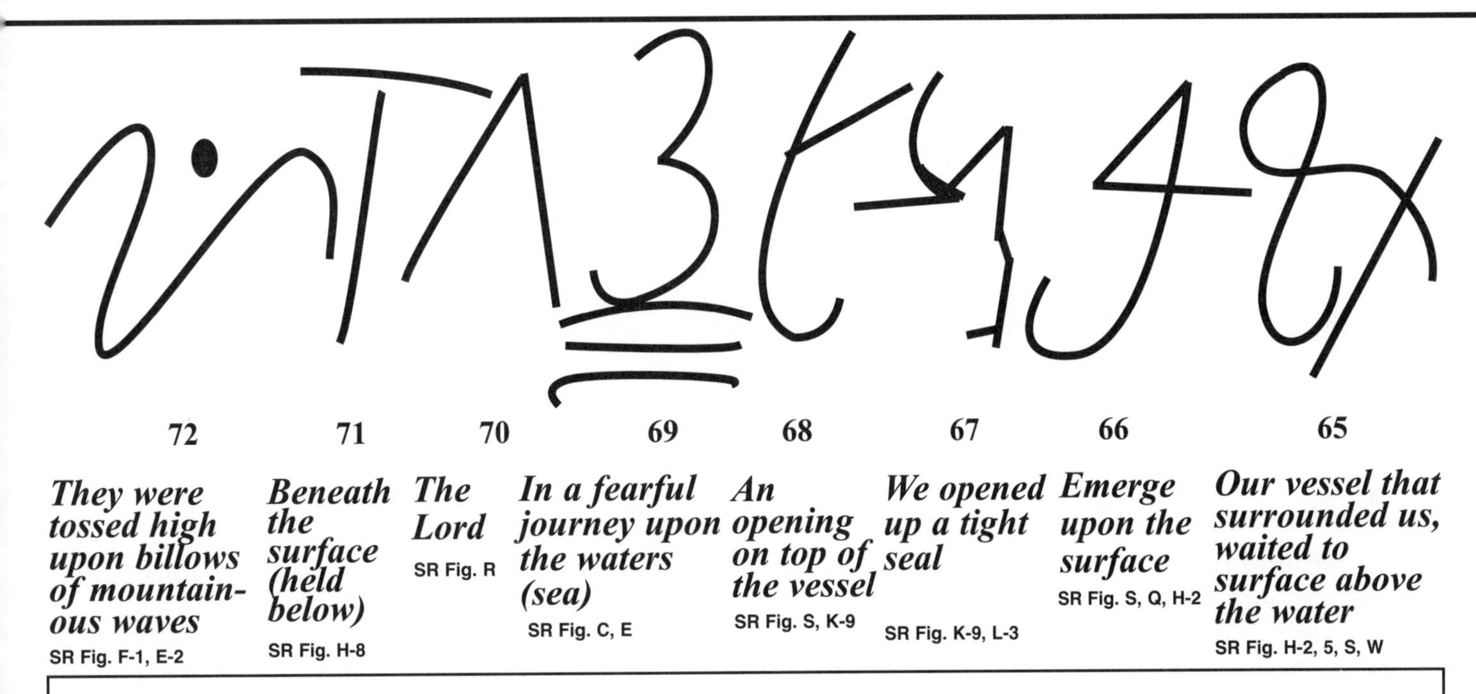

Symbol 65 is a sign incorporation of four symbols: the "vessel below" sign (see Symbol 21) and the Egyptian and Indian sign for "surround," "circuit," "encircle," and in one case "repel" (water) sign (Gardiner, p. 521 V-1, 522 V-7, V-10) and (Martineau, p. 152, chart 6-18). Another part of this sign incorporation is the "surfaced above" sign (see Symbol 15). The "man" sign (see Symbol 9) in the "surfaced above" sign is on an angle to indicate that the people "waited" to surface (Martineau, p. 160, 138, 139) to take in more air into their vessel. The horizontal line indicating "surface" is bent to indicate that the water surface was in the form of waves (and caused their vessel to be tossed about on the sea). **Symbol 66** is the sign incorporation combining the "surfaced above" sign (see Symbol 15) with the sign on an angle to indicate waiting. It is connected to the top of the "surfaced above" sign and the left side of the surface line to depict holding on top of the surface of the water. **Symbol 67** is a sign incorporation depicting a "tight seal" "waiting" to be opened while "staying" on the "surface" . **Symbol 68** is the "vessel" sign (see Symbol 21) with the sign for "open" or "receive" ("daylight and air") on top of the vessel (Martineau, p. 160, chart 8, symbol 4, 116 fig. 60, Symbol 6). **Symbol 69** is the same as Symbol 3 with one addition. The water sign has three lines. The third line is turned down, possibly to say that the voyage was completed (see SR fig. C, E). **Symbol 70** is the same sign as Symbol 46. **Symbol 71** has the sign for "surface" , with the man sign (see Symbol 9, 10). **Symbol 72** is a sign incorporation with the symbol for a "position" that is up over the top of the symbol "great mountainous waves" to indicate that their position was tossed high on billows of mountainous waves.

(Verse 6 cont.) ...and also the great and terrible tempests (13), (26), (32), (35), (42), (51), (75), (76), (82) which were caused by the fierceness (75), (76), (134) of the wind (13), (26), (32), (35), (42), (51), (75), (76) (113), (130), (131).

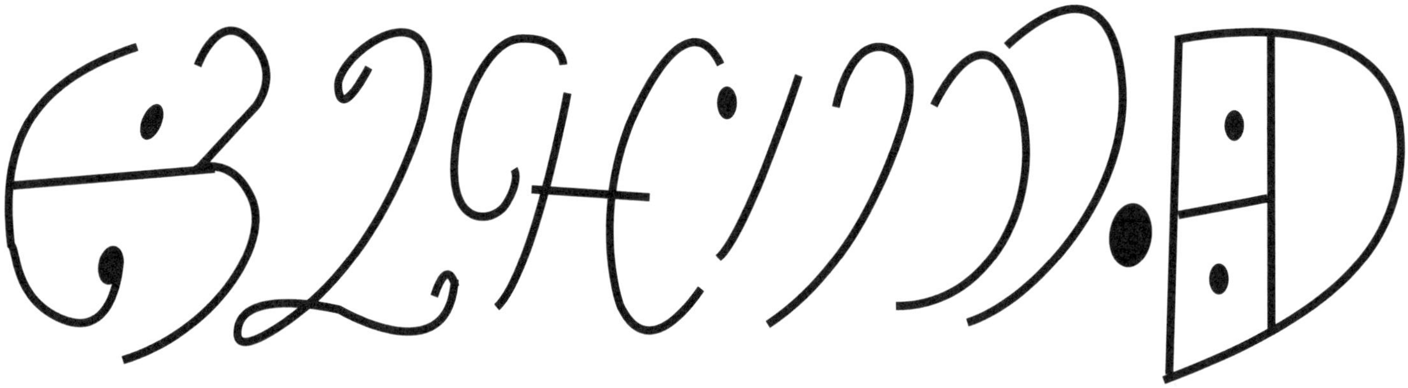

81	80	79	77	76	75	74	73
We were held on a fearful voyage (the Lord took control of our course. The wind and the waves obey his will) SR Fig. C, F-12, K	***We went forth*** SR Fig. G-8	***We had with us in the tight quarters of our vessel the light of day*** SR Fig. B, H-7, K-1	***In this position*** SR Fig. F-1 ***The people*** SR Fig. H-1	***The wind*** SR Fig. A	***Driven forth before tempest-uous winds*** SR Fig. A-3	***In this position*** SR Fig. F-1	***Food in storage being used*** SR Fig. Z, I-4

Symbol 73 is a repeat of Symbol 33. **Symbol 74** is a repeat of Symbol 34. **Symbol 75** is a repeat of Symbol 13. **Symbol 76** is a veering sign and when added to Symbol 75 it becomes a tripled veering sign to add even greater emphasis to the strength of the wind that blew, driving their vessel forth upon the sea. **Symbol 77** is the repeat of Symbol 9. **Symbol 78** is the repeat of Symbol 34. **Symbol 79** is the repeat of Symbol 25, with one exception—the Egyptian hieratic  "legs walking" sign is missing. **Symbol 80** is a repeat of the sign number 30. **Symbol 81** is a sign incorporation with the fear sign described in Symbol 3 and the chamber sign we saw repeated in Symbol 12. They are joined together with the "course" sign we saw in Symbol 10 to denote they were held on this course. The course is running between two position signs to denote going between, on this course (possibly to say that they were being directed by an intelligent power who directed their course).

7. And it came to pass (100) that when they were buried (4), (7), (14), (22), (23), (24), (39), (40), (85), (86), (91), (93), (121), (156) in the deep (22), (39), (85), (86), (91), (121)...

90	89	88	87	86	85	84	83	82
Beneath the surface (held below)	*Our posit ion*	*The Lord*	*We crossed, being driven forth by mighty winds*	*Great waves encompassed us about on this course*	*As we crossed a great sea we were many times submerged on this course*	*Our vessel was sealed over us*	*And it came to pass (came and passed by)*	*The wind*
SR Fig. H-8	SR Fig. F	SR Fig. R	SR Fig. A-5	SR Fig. F-3, E	SR Fig. F-9, H-1, J	SR Fig. S, U, K-9	SR Fig. G	SR Fig. A

Symbol 82 is a "veering" sign. It is a possible repeat of Symbol 1 and Symbol 76. If we could see the line of symbols that preceded the Symbol 1, the last symbol in that line would probably be the "chamber" sign , as we see here with Symbol 81. This sign, together with Symbol 1, would symbolize "narrowing" or "a bad place" (Martineau, p. 124, 125-b). **Symbol 83** is a repeat of the sign "and it came to pass" (see Symbol 5). **Symbol 84** is is the same sign as Symbol 56, only with the "chamber cover" or "hidden" sign attached on the top that we saw in Symbol 54. Attached to the "hidden" sign is the sign for "tight seal"on top, which we saw in Symbol 67. **Symbol 85** is the same sign as Symbol 22. **Symbol 86** is similar to Symbol 40 with only one exception. Note the center dot is being cradled at the bottom of the wave to show how the tempest was raging and how high the billows were tossing. **Symbol 87** is a repeat of Symbol 26. **Symbol 88** is a repeat of the "Lord" (see Symbol 46). **Symbol 89** is the same sign as Symbol 34. **Symbol 90** is identical to Symbol 71.

(Verse 7 cont.) ...there was no water (91) that could hurt them (101), (see symbols 106-116),...

95

The people who came on this voyage

SR Fig. H-1

94

We cried (mouth sign) that we might emerge back upon the surface of the water SR Fig. Y, H-5

93

A long journey under the water's surface

SR Fig. F-9

92

The food in storage being used

SR Fig. Z, I-4

91

The sea opened up and we did emerge beneath billows of mountainous waves SR Fig. F, E-2

Symbol 91 is very much like Symbol 40, only with the three dots (the Indian sign for a weak or fragile trail) in the descending position to symbolize being buried by mountainous waves that drove over them in a storm-tossed sea (Ether 6:6). **Symbol 92** is a repeat of Symbol 33. **Symbol 92** is the repeat of Symbol 33. **Symbol 93** is like Symbol 22, only it zeros in on the long journey stretching across the sea with the four dots (a fragile path), submerged below the surface of the water. **Symbol 94** is the Indian sign to cry (Mallery, vol. I, p. 81, fig. 491) out to the Lord (Symbol 88). The sign over the mouth opening is the rest of the "emergence" sign ┼, indicating that they cried out to the Lord that he might bring them "forth again upon the top of the waters" (Ether 7:6). **Symbol 95** is a repeat of Symbol 9.

(Verse 7 cont.) Their vessels being tight (67), (101) like unto a dish (101), (Ether 1:16-21), and also they were tight like unto the ark of Noah; therefore when they were encompassed about by many waters (101)...

102 *On this course* SR Fig. K-1

101 *Our position was within a dome-shaped vessel, which was encompassed about by many waters* SR Fig. F-7, F-1, W-3, B-2

100 *And it came to pass (came and passed by)* SR Fig. G

99 *Towards* SR Fig. H-10

98 *On this course* SR Fig. K

97 *Stone of crystal (symbol of light)* SR Fig. D

96 *We stayed on this journey in the sea* SR Fig. Zzzz, E, H-3, F-1

Symbol 96 is a sign incorporation of four symbols. "The coil represents something coming down from off the top....The small dot at the top of this symbol represents the point of origin....The line extending from this dot to the coil represents the path" (Martineau, p. 24, fig 15). The people "stayed some time" on this course, "as indicated by a connecting line." (Frank Waters, *Book Of The Hopi* [Harrisonburg: R.R. Donnelley & Sons Company, 1963], p. 103, fig. 46; p. 104, fig.47). "A straight line is used to indicate travel. A waved line is used to indicate travel by sea (Ettie A. Rout, *Maori Symbolism* [London: Harcourt, Brace & Compnay, 1926], p. 159). **Symbol 97** is a repeat of Symbol 2. **Symbol 98** is a repeat of Symbol 10. **Symbol 99** is a repeat of Symbol 20. **Symbol 100** is a repeat of Symbol 5. **Symbol 101** is a sign incorporation describing the vessel in which the people traveled. The dot in the center is the vessel that held them. The cover over them is a dome shape like a kiva. The sign used here is the same Indian gesture for "day" used in Symbol 7, only in reverse. It is when the index and thumb form a circle (remaining fingers closed) and are passed from west to east to depict the convex shape of the sky . The next sign is an Egyptian symbol that means envelop, encircle, bag, bundle, or hold (Gardiner, p. 522, 558). It has the identical meaning among most Indian tribes, and in this context the meaning is that the people on this course were completely "encompassed about by raging waters...that could not harm them" because they were in a "water tight vessel" (note how the "dome cover" sign contacts the "encircle" sign to depict "tight" or "sealed" and the wave-like arms dangling about the left and right side to depict the water that "encompassed them" (Ether 6:7). **Symbol 102** is the same sign as Symbol 10.

(Verse 7 cont.) ...they did cry (109) unto the Lord (118),...

109	108	107	106	105	104	103
Cried (the mouth sign) with anguish of spirit SR Fig. Y	***That the waters brake through*** SR Fig. A-4	***In our course*** SR Fig. K-1	***We had with us in the tight quarters of our vessel the light of day as we went forth*** SR Fig. B, H-7, F-3, G	***Being driven upon a course by a great force*** SR Fig. E, B	***Crossing over*** SR Fig. H-6, K-4	***Covered over in our position*** SR Fig. Zzz, F-1

Symbol 103 is a repeat of Symbol 16. **Symbol 104** is a very common Indian and Egyptian sign for "cross," "within," "in," "interior," "young," or "renewal" (Gardiner, p. 539, Z-10, p. 484 M-42, pp. 462 F-10). It is also the sign for a star in both Indian and Egyptian (Waters, p. 33, fig. 6 and 7). Two signs incorporated signify two opposite shores of the water, and represents "crossover" from one side to the other (Mallery, vol. I, p. 320, fig. 390, fig. 393, p. 331 fig. 438). **Symbol 105** is the same sign as Symbol 51, only without showing their position before the great force of a raging tempest of wind and wave. **Symbol 106** is a repeat of Symbol 25. **Symbol 107** is a repeat of Symbol 10. **Symbol 108** is a sign incorporation showing the water surface entering a "veering" sign (Martineau, p. 160, chart 8, [22]). This is to indicate the water entering into their vessel. (See Symbol 115). **Symbol 109** is a repeat of Symbol 29 with one change: the vertical line under the mouth sign is sharply bent and leaning to show stress or anguish (Martineau, p. 160, chart 8 [17], [16]); Gardiner, p. 497 [O-37]); Ether 6:7 "They did cry unto the Lord").

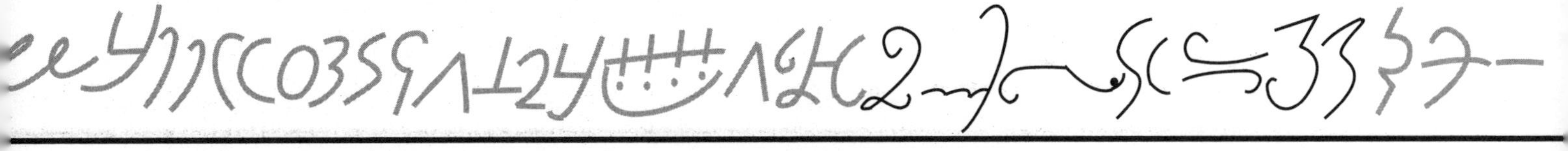

(**Ether 6:7**...there was no water that could hurt them [115, 116],...)

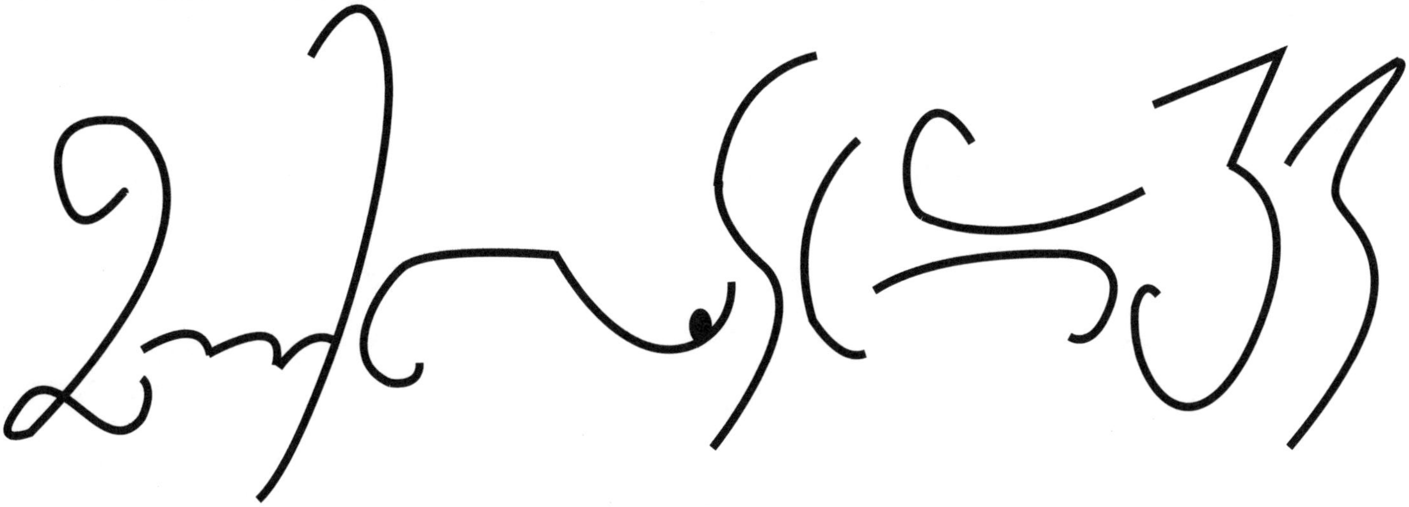

116	115	114	113	112	111	110
We went forth SR Fig. Zzzz, G	***The waters were turned back from entering our place*** SR Fig. A-6	***We were kept dry in this position (a ladle, wet)*** SR Fig. F-1, S-5, Zzzz	***Breathing air*** SR Fig. P	***In Our vessel*** SR Fig. B	***A constant force was upon us, whether we were above or beneath the water*** SR Fig. E, A, B	***Fearful (doubled to add emphasis)*** SR Fig. C

Symbol 110 is a repeat of Symbol 3 without the water sign. It is doubled to add emphasis. There are slight variations in the way they are rendered to give added meaning. **Symbol 111** is the "chamber" sign we saw in Symbol 12, and is attached to the "course" sign we saw in Symbol 10. When rendered this way it depicts the force or current moving the vessel forward. The sign has a double that is turned over to show travel both above and below the surface of the water. The double is facing backwards, possibly to denote the force that was against their vessel. **Symbol 112** is a repeat of the "chamber" sign in Symbol 12. **Symbol 113** is a repeat of the "breathing" sign in Symbol 11. **Symbol 114** is the Indian sign for wet. It is a ladle or dipper (Martineau, p. 26, 27, fig. 17-[a]; p. 92, 93, fig. 48, Symbol 39) and is showing the position of the people within the cup of the dipper to show that they should be getting wet. **Symbol 115** is a sign incorporation with the "water" surface symbol running into the Indian "repel" sign (see Symbol 1). It depicts the idea that the people were not harmed by the sea because their chamber repelled the water. **Symbol 116** is a repeat of Symbol 30 (although it resembles Symbol 43 more).

(Verse 7 cont.) ...and he did bring them forth (120), (121) again upon the top (122), (124) of the waters (119), (122).

124	123	122	121	120	119	118	117
Did bear us up	***The Lord***	***Held on top of the surface***	***We went before the wind on the face of the water***	***Held us up (brought us forth)***	***As we crossed a great sea, we were many times submerged on this course***	***The Lord***	***We had with us in the tight quarters of our vessel the light of day as we went forth***
SR Fig. Q, B, H-1	**SR Fig. R**	**SR Fig. H-9**	**SR Fig. A, K-1**	**SR Fig. Q, T**	**SR Fig. F-9, H-1, J**	**SR Fig. R**	**SR Fig. B, H-7, F-3, G**

Symbol 117 is a repeat of Symbol 25. **Symbol 118** is a repeat of Symbol 46. **Symbol 119** is a repeat of Symbol 22. **Symbol 120** is a sign incorporation combining the "towards" sign described in Symbol 20, and the "came forth" sign described in Symbol 66. They are connected to depict the idea that the Lord who brought them on this journey took control and held them up as they traveled forth on this course (see also Symbol 24). **Symbol 121** is the "wind" sign described in Symbol 13. This sign is joined together to the front end of the "course" sign described in Symbol 10. Joined together like this, they resemble the "went forth" sign described in Symbol 30 and may depict their going forth before the wind that "blew upon the face of the water" (see Ether 6:5). **Symbol 122** is similar to the sign in Symbol 54, only with out the shepherd's crook. **Symbol 123** is a repeat of the Symbol 46. **Symbol 124** is the "chamber" sign depicted in Symbol 12, and is being supported by the "sacred man" sign in Symbol 9, to say that the Lord "did bear them up."

8. And it came to pass (147) that the wind (128) did never cease (130) to blow (129), (128), (131)...

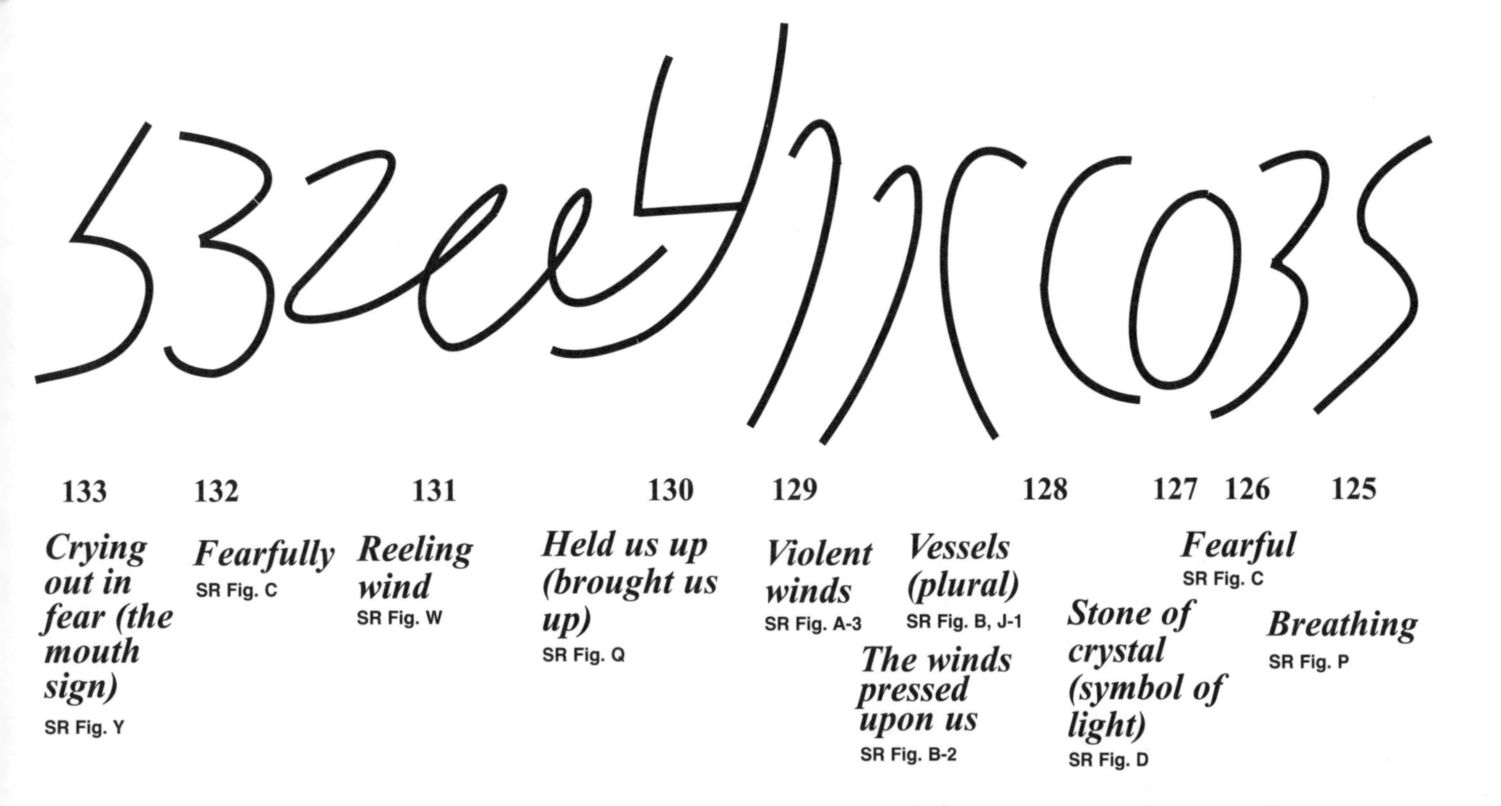

Symbol 125 is a repeat of the "breath" sign in Symbol 8. **Symbol 126** is a repeat of the "fear" sign in Symbol 3. **Symbol 127** is a repeat of Symbol 2. **Symbol 128** is a repeat of Symbol 12, with one exception: it is doubled to indicate that there was more than one vessel on this journey. **Symbol 129** is a repeat of Symbol 13. It is interesting to note that Symbol 129 and Symbol 128 are facing back to back and may be indicating the Indian sign "narrow" or "conflict" (Martineau, p. 106, fig. 53; 124, fig. 64; consolidation no. 10, bridge [b]). "Conflict" describes very well the problem that these people in their vessels had with violent winds. **Symbol 130** is a repeat of Symbol 120, only with slight variations. **Symbol 131** is symbol made up of the Indian and Egyptian sign for "circuit" or encircle (Martineau, p. 152, chart 6 [18]; Gardiner, p. 522, V-7, V-8). They have been doubled to add emphasis. The "wind"sign appears to be attached to the end of two "circuit" signs to denote reeling winds (a raging sea and tempest winds). **Symbol 132** is a repeat of the "fear" sign in Symbol 3. **Symbol 133** is the "mouth" sign with the "leaning over" symbol attached on the top to denote stress (see symbol 109), or fear and crying out (to the Lord [see Symbol 138]).

(Verse 8 cont.) towards (130), (174), (183), the promised land (150), (213) while they were upon (122), (203) the waters (149); and thus they were driven forth before the wind (160).

9. And they did sing praises (137) unto the Lord (138);...

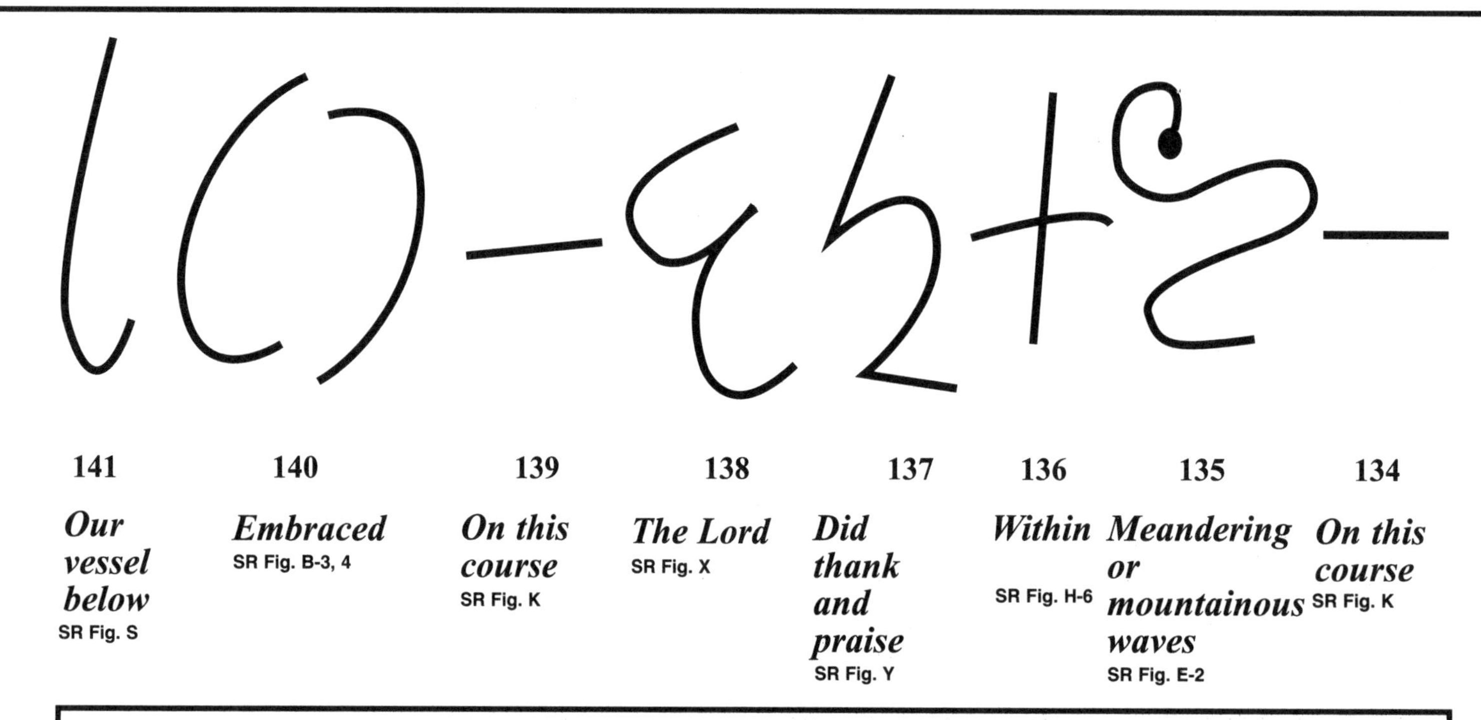

Symbol 134 is a repeat of Symbol 10. **Symbol 135** is a common Indian sign for "path" or "trail." It is a "gone" sign with a "bad" or "crooked" trail. The dot is the position sign and the crooked line is the symbol for bad or a curving path, like the coils of a dangerous snake. The vessels were being tossed high on the billows of a raging sea (Martineau, p. 22, 23, fig. 14-[b, c,], p. 88, 89, fig. 47, symbol 13; p. 94, Symbol 45). **Symbol 136** is a repeat of Symbol number described in Symbol 109 and 133, with one exception: in this case the people's attention is turned to the Lord. They are "thanking" and "praising" Him (138) for their safety and security (140) within (136) their chamber (141) on this fearsome (132) voyage (135), (134). **Symbol 138** is a repeat of Symbol 38. **Symbol 139** is a repeat of Symbol 10. **Symbol 140** is an Egyptian and Indian sign for "embraced" (Gardiner, p. 453, D-32; Martineau, p. 78, 79, fig. 43, Symbol 31). This sign is also similar to the Hopi Indian *nakwach* sign. It is the symbol for friendship and brotherhood. The sign is made when two people literally "embrace" each other's hands in a cupped position (Waters, p. 33 fig. 6 and 7; p. 52, fig. 18); Mallery, p. 643, fig. 1003). **Symbol 141** is a repeat of the "vessel" sign in Symbol 21.

(Verse 9 cont.) ...yea, the brother of Jared did sing praises (145) unto the Lord (242),...

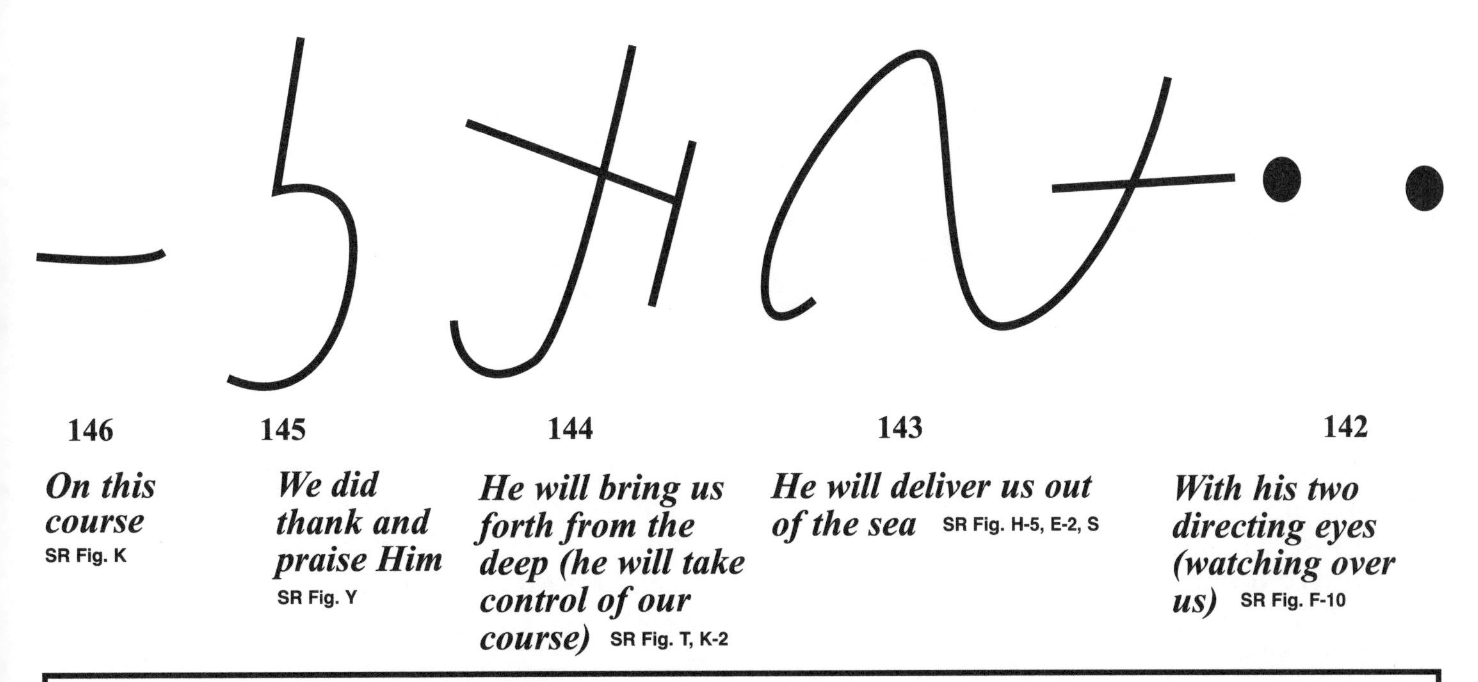

146
On this course SR Fig. K

145
We did thank and praise Him SR Fig. Y

144
He will bring us forth from the deep (he will take control of our course) SR Fig. T, K-2

143
He will deliver us out of the sea SR Fig. H-5, E-2, S

142
With his two directing eyes (watching over us) SR Fig. F-10

Symbol 142 is two dots representing directing eyes. "In Maori the dot indicates that the travellers were God's selected children (in Maori the words are 'the children of God's eye'), and that they were under his eye or under his direction and protection." It is the Egyptian and Indian sign of two watching eyes. It depicts "looking," "all seeing," "watching," and "directing" (*An Egyptian Hieroglyphic Dictionary,* Sir E. A. Wallis Budge, Vol. I, p. cvi, number 14 and 17); Martineau, p. 28, chart 3-A and B; p. 160, chart 8-9 and 13); Rout, p. 161) **Symbol 143** is similar to the sign in Symbol 72 and is showing the billows of mountainous waves. On the left side of the symbol is the "chamber" sign described in Symbol 21. On the right side of the symbol is the "surfaced above" sign described in Symbol 15 to indicate that the Lord will deliver them out of the sea. **Symbol 144** is a sign incorporation with the "coming forth" sign described in Symbol 120, the "surfaced above" sign described in Symbol 15. The Indian and Egyptian sign for "holding firm" is also part of this sign incorporation to depict that the Lord will bring them forth from the deep sea and will take hold of their course (Martineau, p. 98 and 99, fig. 49, symbol 10; p. 160, chart 8, no. 15); Gardiner, p. 443, A-59; p. 445, A-10). **Symbol 145** is the mouth sign resembling the mouth signs described in Symbol 84, 109, 124, 137, only with one exception: the line on top is vertical to denote that the people were in a state of happiness and were thanking and praising the Lord (138). **Symbol 146** is a repeat of Symbol 10.

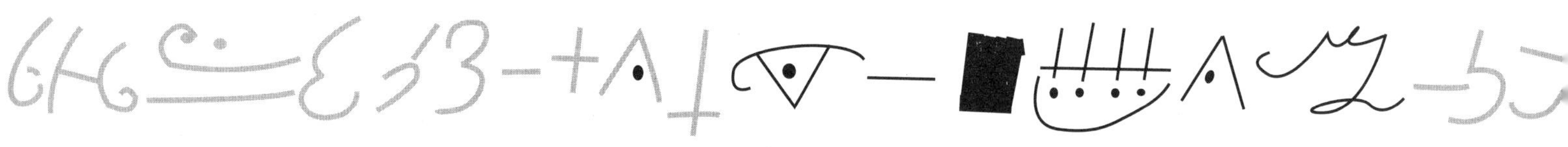

(Verse 7 cont.) ...their vessels being tight (67), (101) like unto a dish (101), (Ether 2:16-21), and also they were tight like unto the ark of Noah; therefore when they were encompassed about by many waters (101), (148).... (Verse **8**) And it came to pass (147) that the wind did never cease to blow (158)...

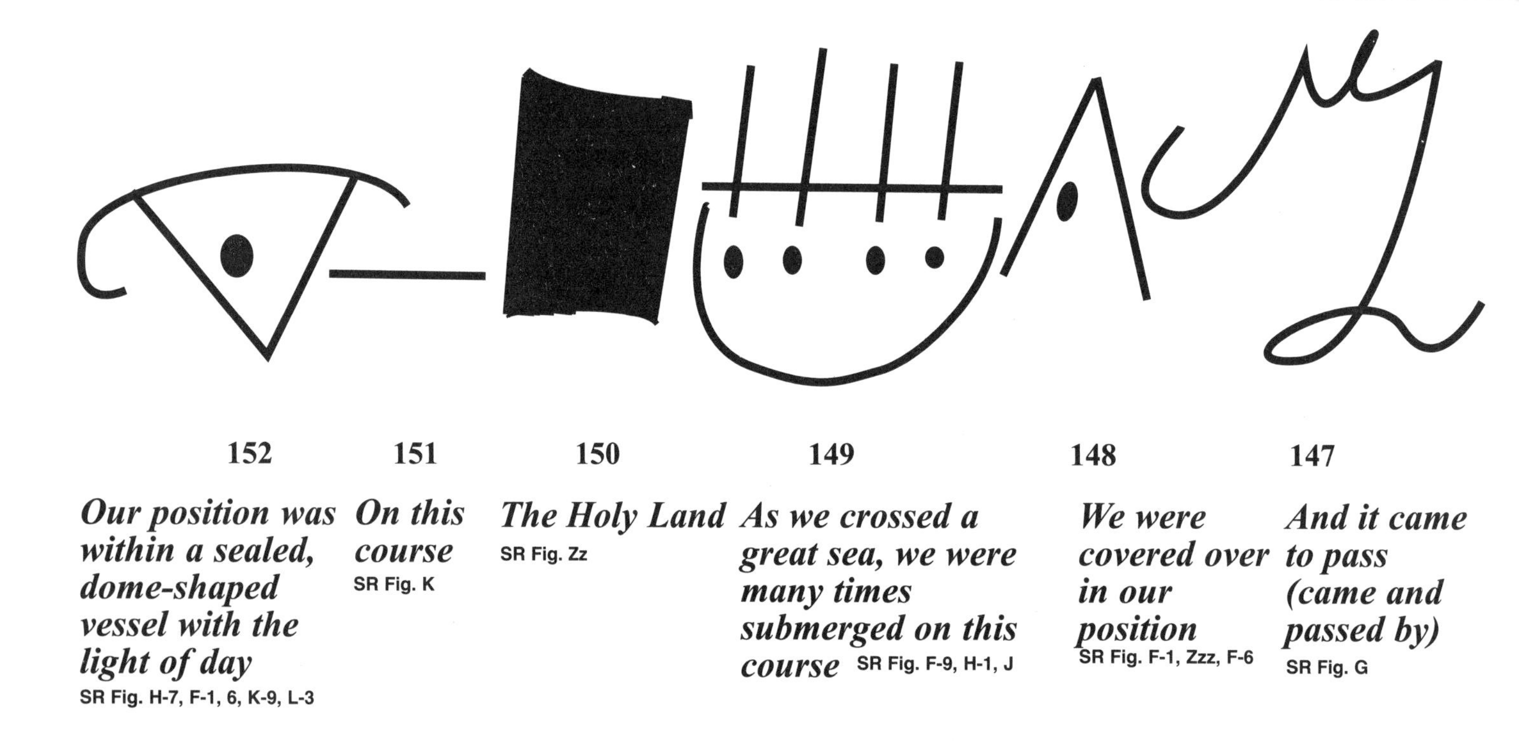

152 ***Our position was within a sealed, dome-shaped vessel with the light of day*** SR Fig. H-7, F-1, 6, K-9, L-3

151 ***On this course*** SR Fig. K

150 ***The Holy Land*** SR Fig. Zz

149 ***As we crossed a great sea, we were many times submerged on this course*** SR Fig. F-9, H-1, J

148 ***We were covered over in our position*** SR Fig. F-1, Zzz, F-6

147 ***And it came to pass (came and passed by)*** SR Fig. G

Symbol 147 is a repeat of Symbol 5. **Symbol 148** is a repeat of Symbol 16. **Symbol 149** is a repeat of the Symbol 22. **Symbol 150** is a repeat of Symbol 44 (see also Symbol 212 and Symbol 213). **Symbol 151** is a repeat of the Symbol 10. **Symbol 15** is a somewhat like the sign in Symbol 101. It too, is a sign incorporation describing the vessel. The dot is in the center of a "V" is to depict that the chamber was filled with light. The "V" is an Indian sign for receive, open, or light. The meaning of this "V" sign is that the people had light in their vessel (Martineau, p. 152, chart 6, no. 7). The cover over them is a dome shape of the sky, or is like a kiva. The sign that is used here is the same Indian gesture sign for "day" (Mallery, p. 694, fig. 1117).

(Verse 8 cont.) ...towards (130), (151), (174), (183) the promised land (150, (213) while they were upon (122), (150), (149), (203) the waters (149); and thus they were driven forth before the wind (160).

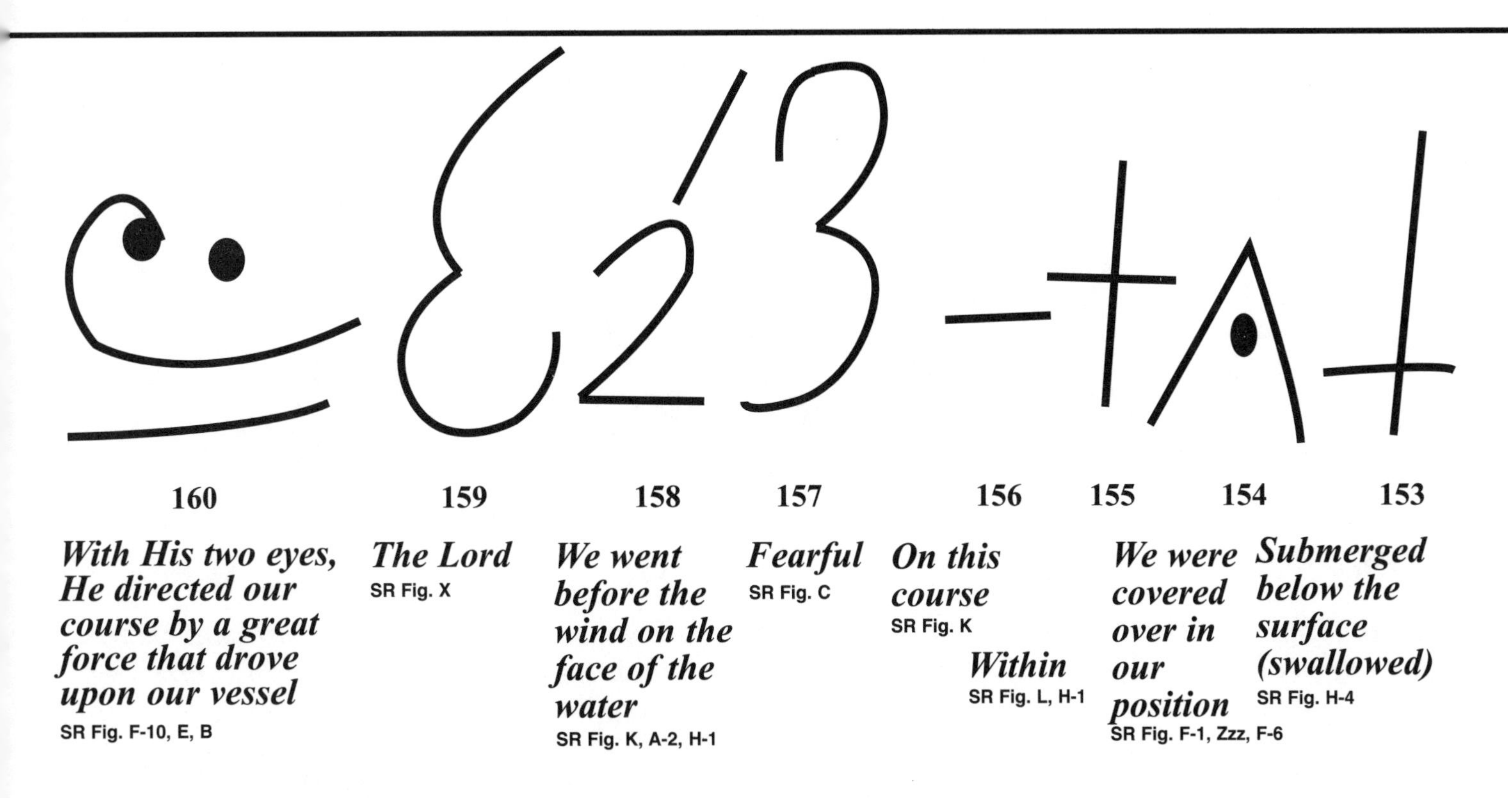

Symbol 153 is a repeat of the Symbol 14. **Symbol 154** is a repeat of the Symbol 16. **Symbol 155** is a repeat of the Symbol 104. **Symbol 156** is a repeat of the Symbol 10. **Symbol 157** is a repeat of the "fear" sign in Symbol 3. **Symbol 158** is a repeat of Symbol 121, only with one addition. A "slanting man" sign is up on top of the sign. **Symbol 159** is a repeat of Symbol 38. **Symbol 160** is a repeat of the Symbol 105 only with one exception. The sign for two directing eyes described in Symbol 242 is part of this symbol incorporation to denote that it was the great directing force of the Lord that was driving them upon this course.

(Verse 9 cont.) ...and he did thank and praise (165), (166) the Lord (159) all the day long (165); and when the night came, they did not cease (165) to praise (165) the Lord (167).

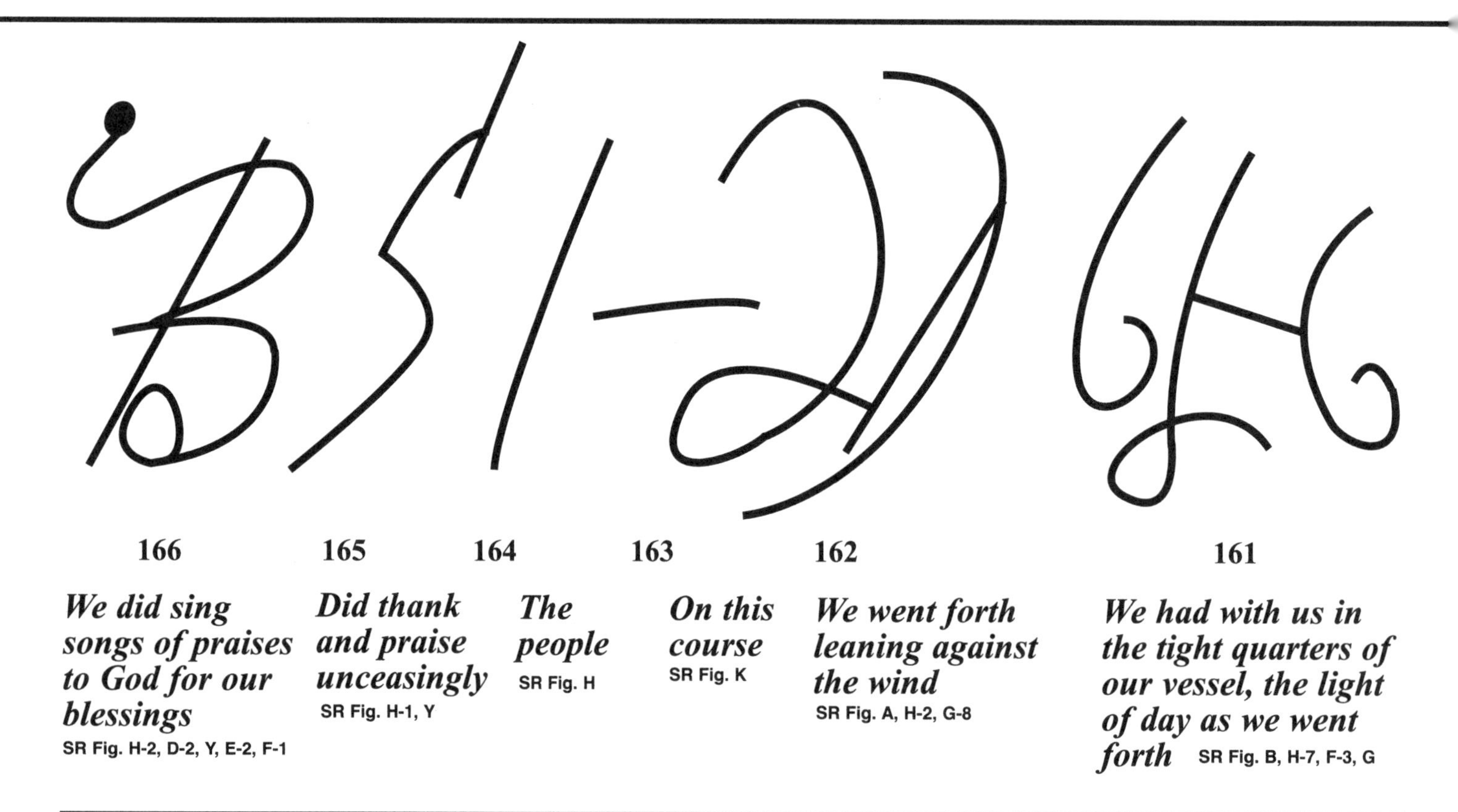

Symbol 161 is a repeat of Symbol 25. **Symbol 162** is a sign incorporation with the "wind" sign described in Symbol 13, and the "leaning" sign described in Symbol 109, which is shown leaning against the "wind" sign. There is also the "went forth" sign described in Symbol 30 which is shown touching the leaning sign. Being attached in this manner is to show that the people on this journey went forth by the strength of the wind. **Symbol 163** is a repeat of Symbol 10. **Symbol 164** is repeat of Symbol 9. **Symbol 165** is a repeat of the "mouth" sign described in Symbol 145 with only one exception. The line on top is vertically arched and attached to a "held on" described in Symbol 144 to denote that the people "did thank and praise the Lord" and they "did not cease to praise" Him (Ether 6:9). **Symbol 166** is a sign incorporation with the mouth sign as described in Symbol 165, only with the "gone" sign on top that was described in Symbol 135. Attached below the mouth sign is the Indian sign for "good medicine" or blessings from heaven (see Mallery, vol. I, Ojibwa Chant, p. 239, "Medicine from the sky;" p. 381, fig. 491, Assimiboin mouth sign). The horizontal line extending down the lateral opening of the mouth is leaning, to indicate that the people sang songs both praising and thanking their Lord unceasingly (165) under this stressful condition (133).

(Verse 5 cont.) ...that the Lord God (38), (167) caused that there should be a furious wind (42), (172) blow upon the face (185), of the waters (40) towards (43) the promised land (44);....

172	171	170	169	168	167
We came forth upon great raging waves on this course SR Fig. K, E-2, B	***Going towards*** SR Fig. G	***We went with the wind*** SR Fig. Q, A-2	***Our position against the wind*** SR Fig. F-1, A-2	***Hidden and held below the surface*** SR Fig. H-8	***The Lord*** SR Fig. R

Symbol 167 is a repeat of Symbol 46. **Symbol 168** is a repeat of Symbol 71. **Symbol 169** is the "veering" or "wind" sign described in Symbol 13. Note the "position" sign cradled within the open side to denote a veering force upon that position. **Symbol 170** is part of the "veering" or "wind" sign described in Symbol 169 with the "towards" sign (see Symbol 20) on the top to depict the great force that carried their vessel towards the holy land (see Symbol 213). Part of **Symbol 171** is the "going towards" sign described in Symbol 8 (It is the Egyptian hieratic sign for "legs walking"). **Symbol 172** is a "wave" sign like the one in Symbol 40. On the left side is the "bring forth" sign described in Symbol 120, and on the right side and bottom is the "course sign" described in Symbol 10 with one exception. The right end is turned down and could be similar to the Maori Indian sign to denote that the voyage was incomplete and was still in progress (Rout, p. 159).

(Verse 5 cont.)...and thus they were tossed upon the waves (72), (179) of the sea (39) before the wind (32), (35), (42), (51), (75), (76), (176), (178), (182)....

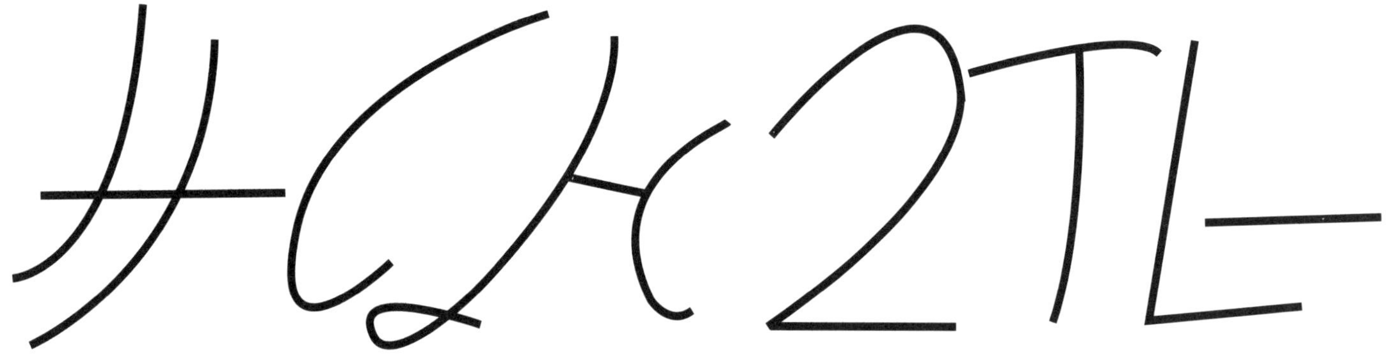

178	177	176	175	174	173
We crossed being driven forth by mighty winds SR Fig. A-5	***We had with us in the tight quarters of our vessel, the light of day, as we went forth*** SR Fig. B, H-7, F-3, G	***We went before the wind on the face of the water*** SR Fig. K, A-2	***Held beneath the surface (hidden from view)*** SR Fig. H-8	***Towards*** SR Fig. H-10	***On this course*** SR Fig. K

Symbol 173 is a repeat of Symbol 10. **Symbol 174** is a repeat of Symbol 20. **Symbol 175** is a repeat of Symbol 71. **Symbol 176** is a repeat of Symbol 121. **Symbol 177** is a repeat of Symbol 25. **Symbol 178** is a repeat of Symbol 26.

(Verse 8 cont.) ...that the wind (180) did never cease (179) to blow towards the promised land (150), (181), (173), (174) while they were upon the waters (176); and thus they were driven forth before the wind (160).... (Verse 10) And thus they were driven forth; and no monster of the sea could break them, neither whale that could mar them; and they did have light (127) continually, whether it was above the water or under the water (190).

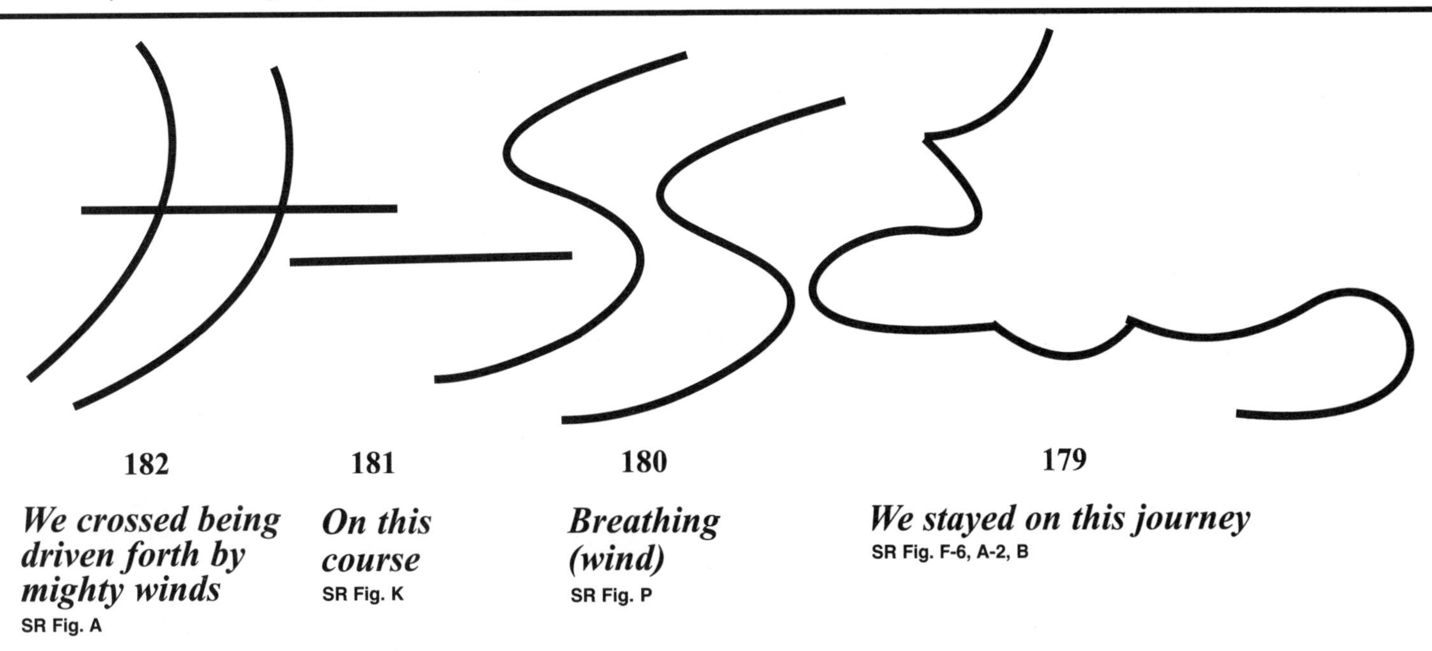

Symbol 179 is is a " stayed on this course upon water" sign, similar to the sign described in Symbol 96. The main difference is that on the right side of this sign the line is curved down. This could be the "wind" sign described in Symbol 13. **Symbol 180** is the "breathing" sign described in Symbol 8, doubled to add emphasis (it could also refer to the wind). **Symbol 18l** is a repeat of Symbol 10. **Symbol 182** is a repeat of Symbol 26.

(Verse 4 cont.) ...commending themselves (37) unto the Lord (38), 81), (189), (191) their God (188).

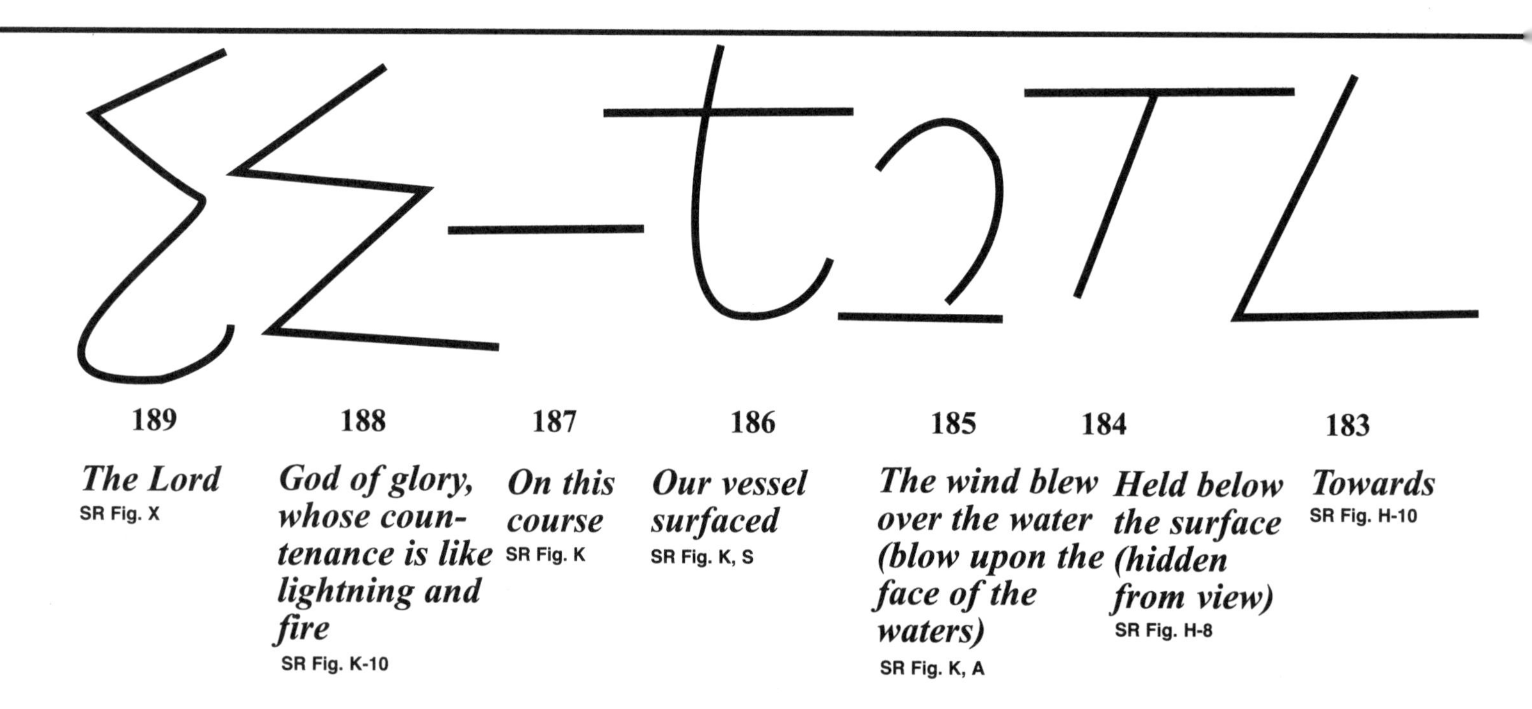

Symbol 183 is a repeat of Symbol 20. **Symbol 184** is a repeat of Symbol 71. **Symbol 185** is the “wind” sign described in Symbol 13. This sign is hovering over the “course” sign described in Symbol 10 to depict the idea “blow upon the face of the waters” (Ether 6:5). **Symbol 186** is a repeat of Symbol 17. **Symbol 187** is a repeat of Symbol 10. **Symbol 188** is the Indian sign for “lightning” and “fire” (Martineau, p. 160, chart 8, number 6; Mallery, vol. II, p. 702). **Symbol 189** is a repeat of Symbol 38.

(Verse 6 cont.) ...that they were many times (22), (48), (59) buried (4), (14), (22), (23), (24), (39, (40), (57), (86), (9l), (190) in the depths (14), (22), (23), (25), (39), (91) of the sea (22), (39), (85), because of the mountain waves (4), (23), (40), (72), (86), (1), (146) which broke upon them (4), (23), (40), (51), (86), (91),...

Symbol 190 is a repeat of the "being driven on a course" sign described in Symbols 111 and 105, only with one addition: the "crossed" sign described in Symbol 57 is part of the incorporation. **Symbol 191** is a repeat of Symbol 46. **Symbol 192** is a repeat of Symbol 10. **Symbol 193** is the sign to be lifted up or carried. **Symbol 194** is the "breathing" sign described in Symbol 8. **Symbol 195** is a repeat of the "breathing" Symbol 193.

(Verse 10) And thus they were driven forth (197), (198);... (Verse 11) And thus they were driven forth, three hundred and forty and four days upon the water (205). (Verse 12) And they did land (199) upon the shore of the promised land (199).

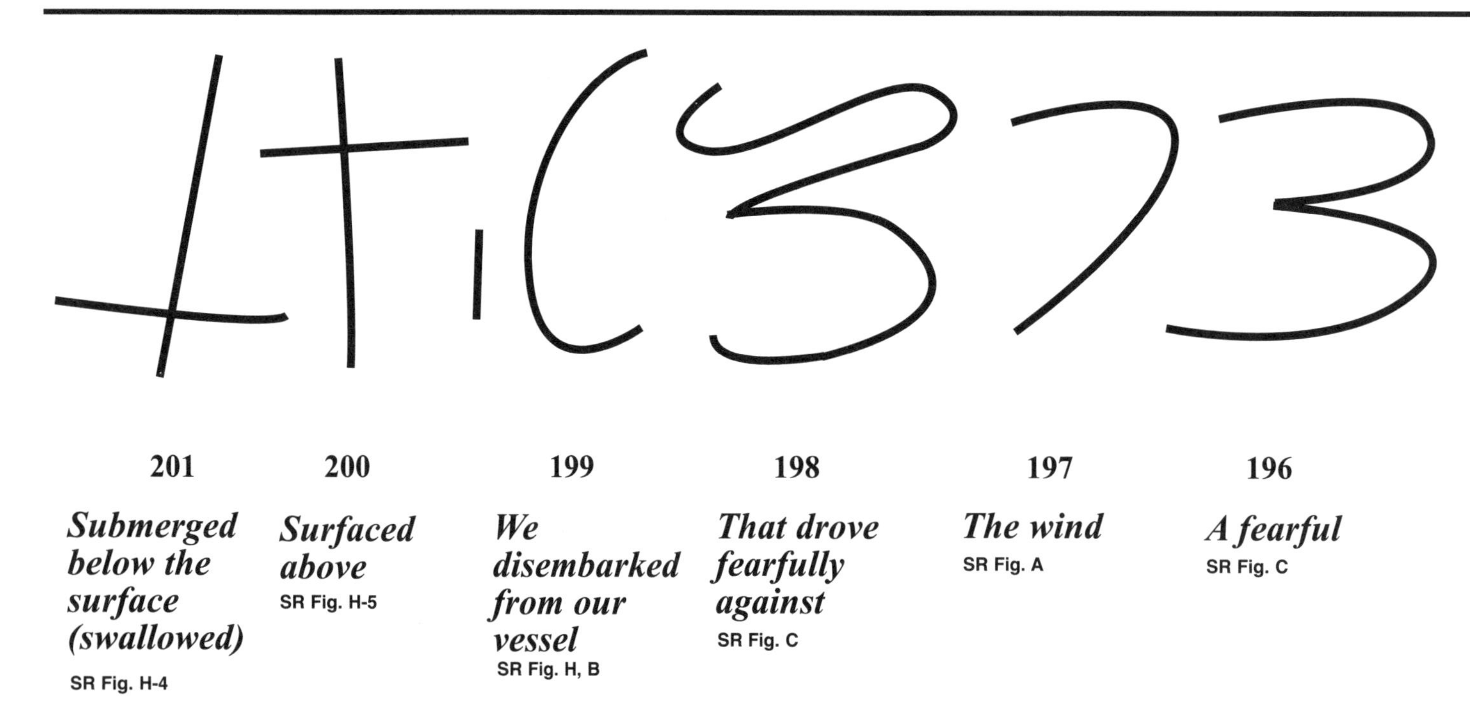

Symbol 196 is a repeat of the "fear" sign described in Symbol 3. **Symbol 197** is the "veering" sign for wind described in Symbol 13. **Symbol 198** is the "fear" sign with the "vessel" sign attached on the top left side. **Symbol 199** is a repeat of the "vessel" sign described in Symbol 12, with the vertical "man" sign on the left side, possibly to suggest disembarking from the vessel at this time. **Symbol 200** is a repeat of Symbol 13. **Symbol 201** is a repeat of Symbol 14. (Note that Symbols 200 and 201 are in reverse order to Symbols 14 and 15, possibly to suggest the end of the voyage.)

Verse 8) ...the wind did never cease to blow (205) towards (207) the promised land (213) while they were upon the waters; and thus they were driven forth before the wind (193-195), (197), (198).

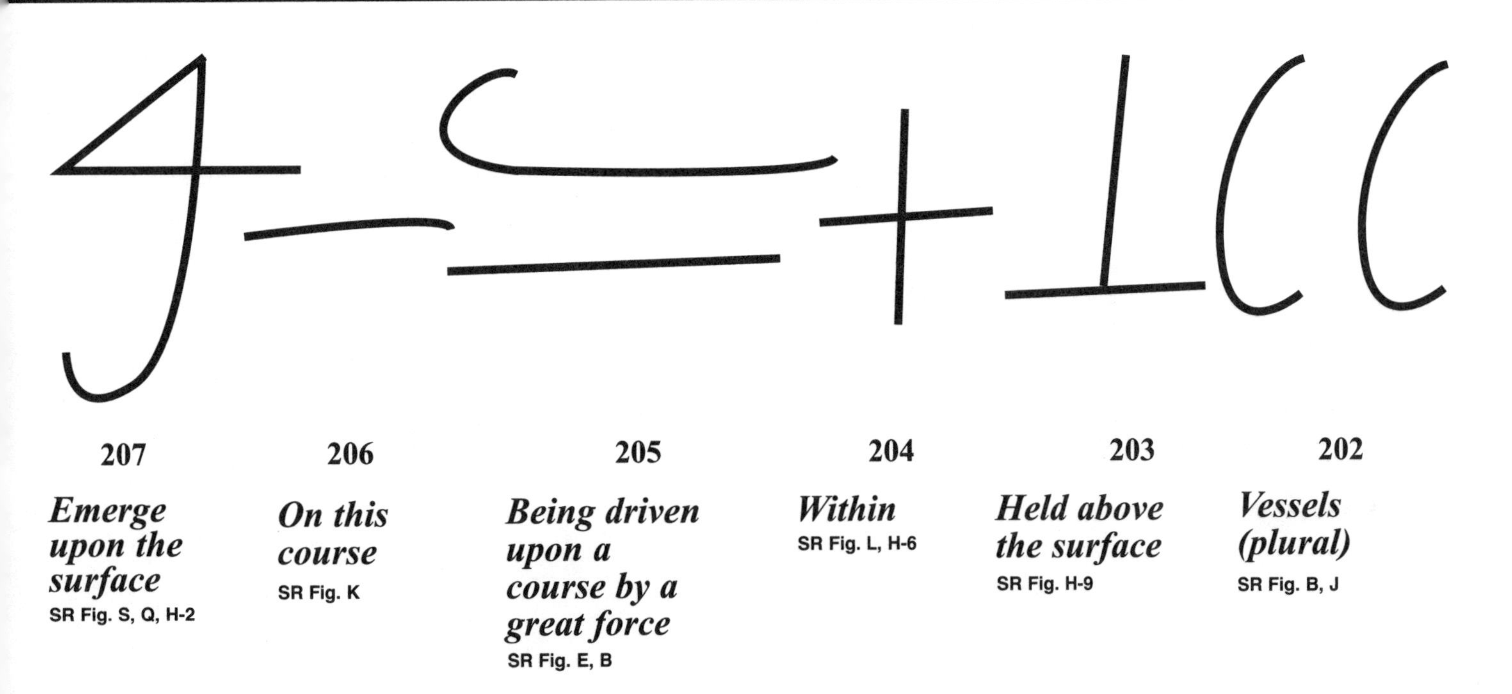

Symbol 202 is the sign for "vessel" and is a repeat of Symbol 128 (see also Symbol 12). **Symbol 203** is the sign for "held on top of the surface" and is similar to the sign in Symbol 54. **Symbol 204** is a repeat of Symbol 136. **Symbol 205** is a repeat of Symbol 51 only with one exception: instead of the "position" sign being in front of this sign, it is the "trail" sign to indicate that the people left the sea behind them. **Symbol 207** is a repeat of Symbol 66 and depicts that the people emerged from their vessels and came onto the land surface.

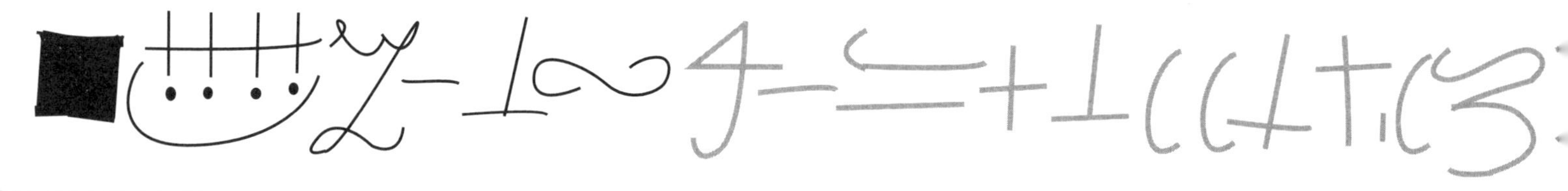

12. And they did land upon (209) the shore (212 and 213) of the promised land (213). And when they had set their feet upon (209) the shores (212 and 213) of the promised land (213) they bowed themselves down upon the face of the land, and did humble themselves before the Lord, and did shed tears of joy before the Lord, because of the multitude of his tender mercies over them.

13. And it came to pass (211) that they went forth (208), (210) upon (209) the face (210) of the land (213), and began to till the earth.

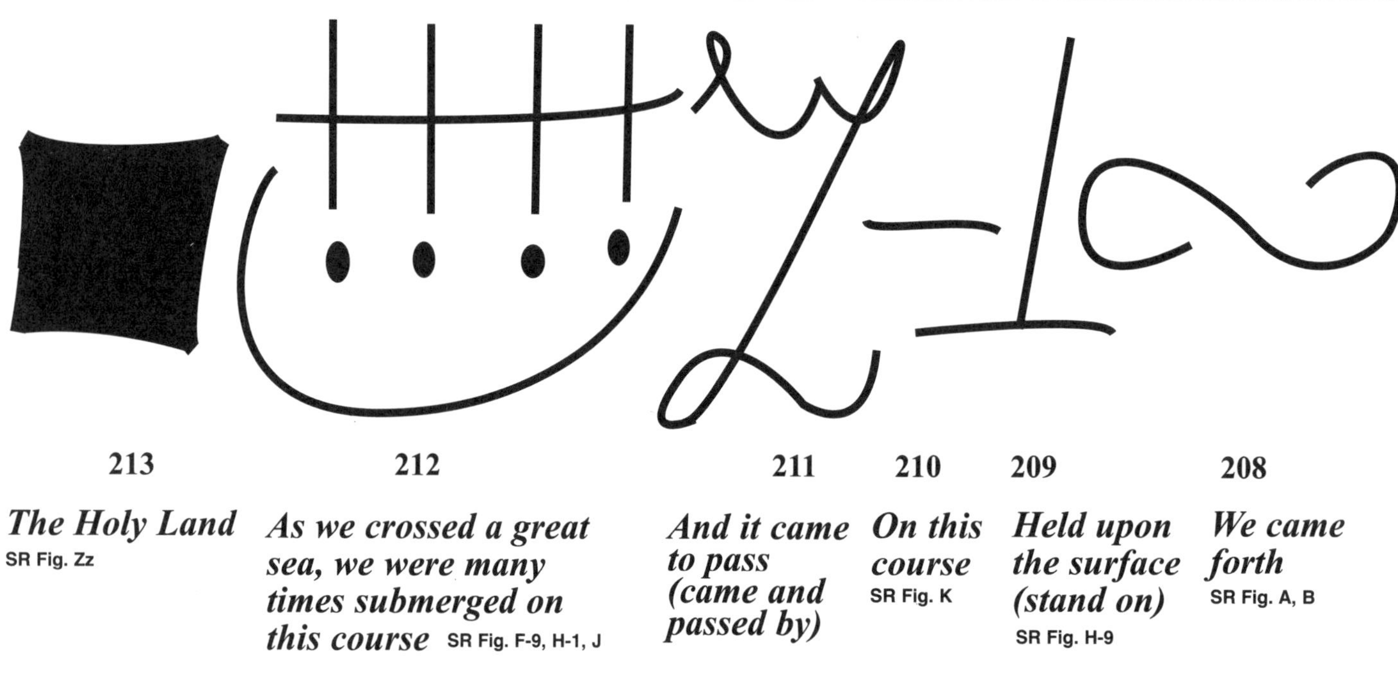

Symbol 208 is a Micmac "mouth" sign and symbolizes an "opening" or "door" or "sing" (Mallery, p. 668, [Gesang]). The "mouth" sign also depicts "opening" or "door" in Egyptian (Gardiner, p. 452, D-16; p. 398 [gate]; see also opening, door, portal, pp. 577, 578, 579 and p. 492, O-1). The Micmac house sign has the "forth" or "from" sign above the house. Note that the Micmac "mouth" sign that depicts "forth" or "from" is rendered in a script "from." The Egyptian house sign is identical to the Micmac house sign. To depict "forth" or "from," the Egyptian mouth sign is added below or . Note that the Egyptian Hieratic "mouth" sign is very similar to the Micmac script rendering of the "mouth" sign (*America B.C.*, Barry Fell, p. 258). **Symbol 209** is a repeat of Symbol 122. This sign at this point in the text, seems to indicate that thy were now held on the land surface. **Symbol 210** is a repeat of Symbol 10**. Symbol 211** is a repeat of Symbol 5. **Symbol 212** is a repeat of Symbol 22. **Symbol 213** is a repeat of Symbol 44. Note that Symbol 212 is next to Symbol 213 like the sea is next to the sea shore (see Martineau, p. 172, fig. 82-d "Arrival of the white man off the East Coast").

THE CONCLUSION

Stan Johnson translated the Anthon Transcript—"reformed Egyptian," using Native American and Egyptian Languages. The translation is the Book of Mormon story of the Jaredite crossing in Ether, Chapter 6.

When we began to write this book, we were incredibly naive. If we had any small clue how much work and sacrifice it would take to actually finish *Translating THE ANTHON TRANSCRIPT,* I'm not sure we would have tried to fit it into our busy lives. At this point we can say it was a labor of love, but definitely a labor. We relate fully to the statement by Neal A. Maxwell, "Mortality has been described by the Lord as being like working in a vineyard— never as an afternoon at a carnival" (*True Believers in Christ,* 136). As the book was brought to fruition, we were able to see the fruit, so to speak, from the vine we had been so carefully and laboriously tending.

When Stan casually began a study of the Anthon Transcript characters, we had not the slightest idea how deeply we would be touched by the affirmations our research provided. Both being regular readers and teachers of the Book of Mormon for many years, we have deep and abiding testimonies that it is the word of God to us in these latter days and that Joseph Smith was the means through which it was translated. Stan has always told his art students to choose pure, good, and righteous subjects with which to work because we learn to love that with which we spend our time. Since writing this book, we have an extra portion of love for the Prophet Joseph Smith, as well as the Book of Mormon. We wish it were possible to write or tell what is in our hearts. Our mouths and minds simply cannot tell you all we know. The best we can wish for you is that you "feast on the words of Christ" (2 Nephi 31:20; 32:3) in this most correct book (the Book of Mormon) on earth, and find out "the peace of God, which passeth all understanding" (Philip. 4:7), by knowing the truth for yourself.

We've presented the facts. We know how much our testimonies have been reinforced through our research. Now it is up to every reader to draw their own conclusion. When Stan told Hugh Nibley, "I used the Indian [Native American] languages as the basis for the translation." Dr. Nibley said, "It is the only sane thing to do." Dr. Nibley has done decades of research on the Book of Mormon, ancient languages, Native American languages and the Jaredites. He was able to draw his conclusion from his own vast resources of information as well as from Stan's translation. We truly hope we've provided enough "plausible evidence" to strengthen your testimony, knowing all the while that faith is vital to really know the truth of all things. Neal A. Maxwell says it so well:

> It is my opinion that all the scriptures, including the Book of Mormon, will remain in the realm of faith. Science will not be able to prove or disprove holy writ. However, enough plausible evidence will come forth to prevent scoffers from having a field day, but not enough to remove the requirement of faith. (*Precious Things,* 4)

APPENDIX

SYMBOL REFERENCE

This section shows the Egyptian and Native American symbols Stan used to translate the Anthon Transcript. He has painstakingly and thoroughly documented each of the 213 symbols in the Anthon Transcript. Each and every one is shown to be a well established ancient sign.

IDEOGRAMS OR SENSE-SIGNS

INDIAN PICTOGRAPHY-SYMBOL INCORPORATIONS

These are signs which show their meaning pictorially.

MICMAC AND MAORI HIEROGLYPHIC

Most people are unfamiliar with the fact that the Native Americans used horizontal writings. The early French trappers, Spanish conquerors, and English explorers were astonished to learn that the "Indians" indeed expressed themselves in writing. These are examples of such writings.

Symbol Reference

Fig. A The Indian veering or end sign to depict the notion of repel, or go around (see symbol numbers 1, 13, 26, 32, 35, 42, 75, 82, 87, 108, 115, 129, 140, 162, 169, 182, 185, and 197).

1. The Egyptian sign for end of years. (*An Egyptian Hieroglyphic Dictionary*, E. A. Wallis Budge, vol. II, p. 703, **sa.**).

2. The first symbol in the text is the Indian "veering" or "repel" sign and in this situation relates to wind, and denotes a bad place to be **(see Symbol 82).***(The Rocks Begin To Speak*, LaVan Martineau, p. 160, chart 8 [22]).

3. **This Indian** sign can be doubled to add the meaning "good," or "wiping clean," nothing there. (Martineau, p. 81, fig. 45, symbol f).

4. Indian sign for break through, penetrate. A course sign penetrating a repel sign **(see Symbol 108).**

5. Indian sign for break through, penetrate. A course sign penetrating two repel signs **(see Symbols 26, 32, 42, 87, and 187).**

6. Indian Sign for repel the water. Repel, veering, or to go around, water resistant (**see Symbol 115**).

Fig. B The Indian veering or end sign to depict the notion of repel, or go around (see Symbols 1, 12, 25, 41, 79, 81, 106, 112, 117, 128, 140, 177, 199, and 202).

1. Egyptian Back; hinder parts; the west; the back door; at the back door. (Budge, vol. II, p. 633, **sa.**)

2. The Indian sign for narrow. Two veering or end signs facing back to back **(see Symbols 128, 129).** (Martineau, p. 124; 125, fig. 64, engine (a), and bridge (b).

3. The Indian sign for "embrace" or (Micmac) "not" Two veering or end signs facing front to front. (Martineau, p. 124; 125, fig. 64, engine (a), and (bridge (b).

4. Hopi Indian sign for embraced hands. It is the Hopi *nakwaach* symbol which depicts friendship and brotherhood. The sign is made when two people literally embrace each others hands in a cupped position (**see Symbol 140**).

Micmac

Akkadian

5. The Micmac Indian and Akkadian sign for "Lord" or "Our Father." A wooden rooftree or pillar scepter of heaven, with two veering or end signs denoting the Micmac "embrace the straight path," and the Akkadian "straight and narrow path leading up" **(see Symbol 140).** (*Picture-Writing of the American Indians,* Garrick Mallery, page 663, fig. 1080, symbols **c**, and **d**; p. 669, fig. 1083 "Our Father"; Martineau, p. 78, 79, fig. 43, Symbol 31; see also Budge,vol. I, p. 507, [heh] Ra, holding scepters of the of the East and West horizons).

Arapaho

6. The Indian sign for the ladder and horizon and the place of emergence. A wooden rooftree or pillar scepter of heaven. Note also the two directing eyes. *(The Arapaho by Alfred L. Kroeter, Vol XVIII, plate XXVI, # 71; plate XXX, # 320).*

Fig. C Fear, evil, in.

1. Micmac. The Micmac Indian sign for fear evil or "in." It is seated upon the Indian and Egyptian symbol for "water" to indicate a fearful course on the sea (**see Symbols 3, 63).**

2. **This Micmac** sign is repeated, or incorporated with some slight variations in **Symbols 3, 37, 69, 81, 110** (*Egyptian Grammar,* Sir Alan Gardiner, p. 469, G-18), 126, 132, 157, 196, 198).

3. Micmac. The Micmac Indian sign for "had it printed" (with ink on paper and a press). The "fear" or "evil" sign is attached to the "course sign" on the left and the "held top and bottom" sign on the right. The "going down stream" sign is to the far right to depict the printer's ink. The literal translation would then be "the paper was held 'in' a fearful course and pressed between on both sides with ink" (Mallery, vol. II, p. 668).

4. Micmac. The Micmac Indian sign for fearful course (**see Symbol 37).** It is the "fear" sign with the "course" sign attached on the right side.

5. Micmac. The Micmac Indian sign for "evils" (Mallery, Vol. II, p. 669, fig. 1083, "The Lord's Prayer in Micmac Hieroglyphics").

6. Egyptian. An Egyptian hieratic barn owl. This is the sign for "I," "in," and "therein," and is linked with combinations dealing with the nightsun, death, the Egyptian resurrection, and the underworld ("in fear," "in death," "under," "below," "from"). (Gardiner, p. 469, G-17, 18; pp. 29, 30, 40, 553, 592, 567, 568, 584, 610, 612).

7. Egyptian An Egyptian hieroglyphic composite "in fear of death" (Gardiner, p. 612).

Fig. D A stone of crystal-symbol of light (see Symbols 2, 55, 61, 97, 127, and 166).

1. Navajo. "Crystals…are symbolic of light, fire, and truth and are used ceremonially to light prayer sticks. In many legends they provide both illumination and fire" (*Southwestern Indian Ceremonial*, Tom Bahti, pp. 8,9).

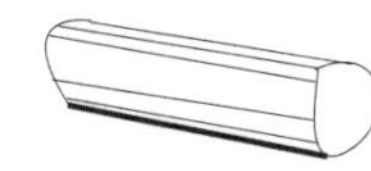

2. Ojibwa "I am taking (gathering) medicine to make me live. The disks indicate the sacred objects sought for, which are successively obtained by the speaker, who represents the officiating shaman" (Mallery, vol. 1, p. 238).

3. Egyptian. Matter, substance, ball, tablet. (Budge, vol. I, p. 651; Gardiner, page 490, N-33).

4. Egyptian. Metallic (shiny) substance (Budge, vol. I, p. 130).

Symbol Reference

Fig E. Water, river, lake, sea, liquid, two banks, swept clean, not on the water.

1. Maori Indian sign for ripple or water (slow movement). "A straight line is used to indicate travel. A waved line is used to indicate travel by sea (*Maori Symbolism Report,* Ettie A. Rout, p. 159).

2. Micmac Indian sign for great mountainous waves. "The mountains skipped" (earthquake) like rams. (See *America B.C.,* Barry Fell, p. 274-b, Psalms 114:4). This sign is shown repeated with a slight variation in **Symbols 4, 40, 72, 86, 91, 135, 143, 172 and 179.**

3. In Maori symbolism, The wavy lines indicate a long continuous sea voyage (Rout, p. 159).

4. Maori Indian sign for water. Three lines indicate migration by water. The two outside lines are two banks or shores. The line going down the middle depicts the path going through or between (Rout, p. 162).

3. Micmac. The Micmac Indian sign for "had it printed" (with ink on paper and a press). The "fear" or "evil" sign is attached to the "course sign" on the left and the "held top and bottom" sign on the right. The "going down stream" sign is to the far right to depict the printers ink. The literal translation would then be, "the paper was held "in" a fearful course and pressed between on both sides with ink" (Mallery, vol. II, p. 668).

6. Navajo Indian sign for the Rio Grand River (fast movement). The line down its center means passing through or floating down *(Martineau,* p. 101, fig. 49, Symbol 34).

7. This Micmac water sign appears repeated, using either one line, two lines, or three lines, and in some situations incorporated in **Symbols 3, 4, 7, 8, 10, 14, 15, 17, 22, 23, 24, 25,26, 28, 31, 32, 37, 39, 40, 41, 42, 45, 48, 49, 50, 51, 52,54, 57, 59, 66, 67, 69, 72, 81, 85, 86, 87, 90, 91, 93, 94, 96, 98, 102, 104, 105, 106, 107, 108, 111, 115, 117, 119, 122, 134, 136, 139, 143, 144, 146, 149, 153, 155, 156, 160, 161, 163, 172, 173, 175, 177, 178, 181, 182, 184, 185, 186, 187,188, 190, 192,200, 201, 203, 204, 206, 207 and 212.**

8. In Maori symbolism, a straight line is used to indicate travel. A waved line is used to indicate travel by sea. When the last curve is downward, that indicates that the journey is unfinished. The four lines here indicate four different halting places (Rout, p. 159).

9. Egyptian water ripple. Ripple of water replaces the sign of land.

10. Egyptian two water ripples. Used as a substitute for the Egyptian "not" (see Gardiner, p. 490, N-35).

11. Egyptian three water ripples. Used linked with combinations dealing or connected with water or liquid. Hence, river, lake, sea (Gardiner, p. 490, N-35, 36).

Fig. F. Course, journey, tracks, footprints (see Symbols 4, 22, 16, 23, 24, 33, 34, 40, 51, 64, 72, 73, 74, 81, 85, 86, 89, 91, 92, 93, 96, 101, 103, 113, 119, 134, 142, 148, 149, 152, 154, 160, 166, 169, 212).

1. An Indian position sign. This dot represents a moccasin track or a position. More than one dot represents tracks or moccasin prints.

2. Ontario, Canada (Indian pictograph). The base line has been made into two elk. One of the two elk is a calf, indicating that the group was made up of men women and children. They were to merge with the main body who were also traveling, indicated by the heavier dots.

3. This Indian sign,depicting a course encompassed about by great, mountainous waves or a journey under the water's surface, is repeated, or incorporated, with some slight variations in **Symbols 4, 22, 40, 85, 93, 119, 149 and 212.**

4. An Indian "gone" sign. The vertical movement line with a dot at the top indicates gone in the Indian pictography **(see Symbols 96, 135, and 166).** (Martineau, p. 160, chart 8, no. 14).

5. A Mayan word meaning "that which is brought down." "The dot in Indian pictography means *here*, and the *movement lines* reaching up over the top of the *position* symbol clearly depict, in a pictographic manner, *brought down from above*. The *arc* over the dot indicates the palm of the hand clutching or covering the dot, and the '*wavy line* pointing downward' indicates that both the hand and the positioned object were brought down" (Martineau p. 144, fig. 77-a).

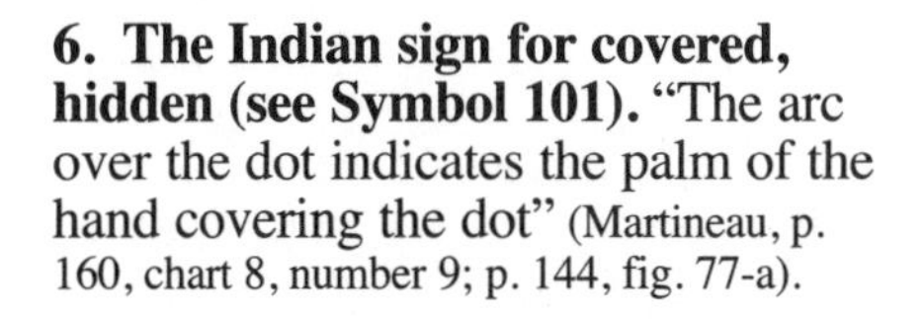

6. The Indian sign for covered, hidden (see Symbol 101). "The arc over the dot indicates the palm of the hand covering the dot" (Martineau, p. 160, chart 8, number 9; p. 144, fig. 77-a).

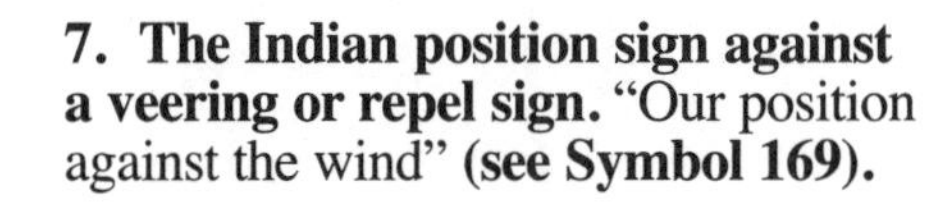

7. The Indian position sign against a veering or repel sign. "Our position against the wind" **(see Symbol 169).**

8. The Indian position sign at the bottom of a bowl (See Symbol 114). (Martineau, p. 56, fig. 36; p. 94 , fig.47, no. 14.)

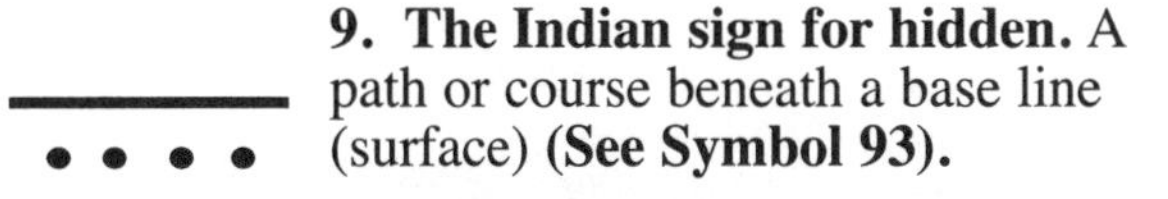

9. The Indian sign for hidden. A path or course beneath a base line (surface) **(See Symbol 93).**

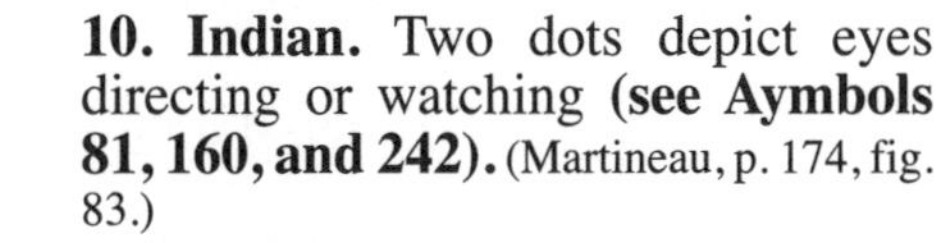

10. Indian. Two dots depict eyes directing or watching **(see Aymbols 81, 160, and 242).** (Martineau, p. 174, fig. 83.)

11. Indian fear. Two eyes hiding beneath a base line (Martineau, p.174, fig. 83).

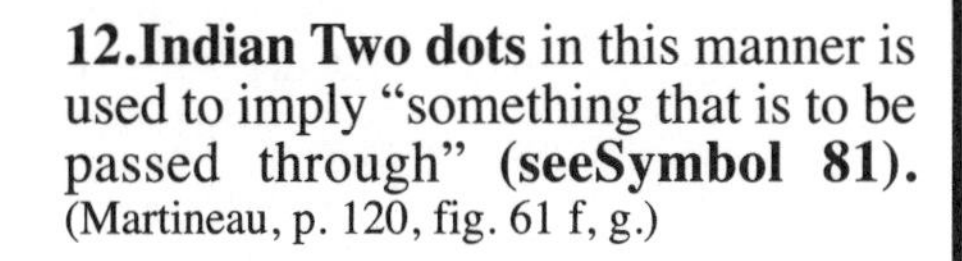

12. Indian Two dots in this manner is used to imply "something that is to be passed through" **(seeSymbol 81).** (Martineau, p. 120, fig. 61 f, g.)

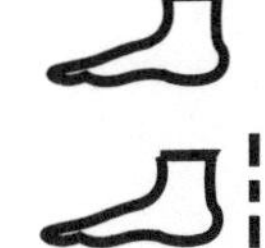

13. Egyptian footprint, place, position; **Egyptian** footprints, plural (Gardiner p. 457, D 58).

Symbol Reference

Fig. G. Plurality, doubling as in two parts, separate (see Symbols 5, 27, 36, 83, 100, 147 and 211). (See Martineau, pp. 50, 51, fig. 30, symbol a.)

Variant Hieratic forms *(from the Book of the Dead.)*

      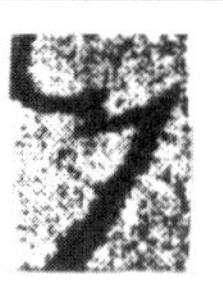

Variant forms of the same character from the Anthon Transcript. (*Improvement Era*, February, 1942)

1. The Indian duality sign over a leg. This sign incorporation depicts the idea of a broken leg. "There were a great many accidents and some legs were broken. The ground being covered with ice (American Horse's winter count, 1847-48). Here the fracture is very obvious-too much so to be intended as objective-rather delineating the idea of the breaking and separation of the bone." (Mallery, vol. II p. 717, fig. 1191).

2. A Paiute Indian recorded his impressions of his train trip back East and used symbols from both old and modern cultures. Appearing directly below the goat between the two train cars is the duality or doubling sign to denote nothing there, taking it off, and other similar meanings. Here it is saying that the train cars could be disconnected (Martineau, p. 50, fig 30, symbol a).

3. The Indian sign "and it came to pass." This sign is identical to the Egyptian hieratic sign with the duality sign over the "legs walking" sign **(see Symbols 5, 27, 43, 83, 100, 147 and 211).**

4. Egyptian hieroglyphic duality sign as in two parts (two diagonal strokes). (Gardiner, p. 536, Z-4.)

5. Egyptian hieratic duality sign as in two parts (two diagonal strokes). (Gardiner, p. 10-D.)

6. Egyptian hieroglyphic duality sign with pool sign and the legs walking sign. This combination depicts the idea to pass by (the pool), surpass (Gardiner, p. 590).

7. Egyptian hieroglyphic duality sign over the legs walking sign. This combination depicts the idea to "travel," "seek" (to "pass by"). (Gardiner, pp. 457, D-54, 582, 624, 627.)

or

or

8. The Egyptian hieratic duality sign over the "legs walking" sign. This combination depicts the idea to "travel," "seek" (to "pass by"). They can be joined together, making one continuous stroke, without lifting the pen to make the sign identical to the Anthon transcript sign in **Symbols 5, 27, 43, 83, 100, 147 and 211** (Gardiner. p. 10-D).

Fig. H. The "man" sign, a figure of a man minus all appendages, numeral one, a pointing finger to indicate direction (Martineau, p. 17, locator [b]).

1. The Maori and Egyptian sign for man (see Symbols 6, 7, 9, 20, 63, 77, 95, 99, 122, 164, 166, 174, and 183). The vertical line is a substitute for a human figure minus all appendages (considered magically dangerous). (Gardiner, p. 537, Z-5).

2. Indian and Egyptian sign for stopped, waiting, leaning or falling (see Symbols 11 and 162). (Martineau, p. 78, fig. 43, Symbol 32; p. 138, chart 5, Symbol 11; Gardiner, p. 497, O-37; Budge vol. I, p. 545, Khefthernebst).

3. The Indian and Egyptian sign for distant or foreign. It is also a Hopi connecting line for "stayed" (see Symbols 67, 96, and 179). (Martineau, p. 160, chart 8, symbol 17; Gardiner, p. 442, sect. A-1; p. 513, T-14; Book of the Hopi, Frank Waters, p. 103,104, fig 46, Gila Bend and Mesa Verde, Speringerville and Chichen Itza).

4. The Indian and Egyptian sign for "cross below the surface in the water or in the earth (swallowed), gone from sight, went under. The vertical line is a motion sign symbolizing a downward direction. The horizontal line at the bottom of the sign indicates a path or course crossing beneath a base line (surface) **(see symbol 7, 14, 57, 153, 190, and 201).** (Martineau, p. 75, fig. 43, symbol 12; 103, fig. 50, symbols 29 and 30; Gardiner, p. 626 [swallow]).

5. The Indian and Egyptian sign for "cross above the surface into the sky (heaven) or to come forth from below the surface. The vertical line is a motion sign symbolizing an upward direction and is crossing above the surface. The horizontal line at the top of the sign is the surface symbol and can also be a (sky band). This sign is often referred to as Mayan "tree of life" symbol or a "Jacob's Ladder" (Gen. 28:12-15). **(See symbol numbers 15, 31, 45, 52, 57, 94, 144, 186, 190, and 200).** (Martineau, p. 112, fig. 57, symbol h; Budge, p. 91, [Astes]; p. 19, [aabtt]; p. 279, [maquet, "the Ladder" whereby Osiris ascended into heaven; p. 361, Neb Maqt Horus of the ladder).

6. Indian and Egyptian sign for crossed, within, star, place of emergence, four cardinal directions, young, renewal (see Symbols 8, 36, 108, 155, and 204. Symbol 9; Waters, p. 113-115; Gardiner, p. 539, Z-10; 462, F-10; 484, M-42; 487, N-14; Budge, p. 172, [Uritamit Tuat]; p. 170 [untuit]).

7. "A common Indian gesture for 'day' is when the index and thumb form a circle (remaining fingers closed) and are passed from east to west) [See Symbols 7, 25, 28, 41, 79, 101, 117, 152, 161, and 177]. In Owens Valley, California, there is a pictograph with a similar sign and was reported in the Ann. Rep. Georg. Survey West of the 100th Median for 1876, Washington, 1876, pl. opp. p. 326, in which the circle may indicate either day or month (both these gestures having the same execution), the course of the sun or moon being represented perhaps in mere contradistinction to the vertical line, or perhaps the latter signifies one" (or the vertical line signifies the man making the sign). (Mallery, vol. II, p. 698, fig. 1132; Budge, p. 163, [upsh]).

8. The Indian and Egyptian sign for east door, beneath or under (see Symbols 71, 90, 168, 175, and 184). The vertical line is the man sign or a ladder or path held below the horizontal base line (surface). (Martineau, p. 28, chart 3, Symbol A; 160, chart 8, Symbol 6, 5; Gardiner p. 496, 0-32; Budge, p. 18-19; p. 474 [heb]; p. 314 [mer]; p. 158 [ubat]; p. 212, [baa]).

9. The Indian sign for standing above or on top of the surface (see Symbols 122, 185, 203, and 209). (Martineau, p. 112, 113, Fig,57, symbol c).

10. The Maori sign for "I am going toward." The vertical line is the sign of man. The horizontal line at base of vertical line indicates travel **(see Symbols 6, 19, 20, 24, 66, 120, 130, 170, 174, 183, and 207).** (Mallery, vol. I, p. 331, fig. 438.)

Symbol Reference

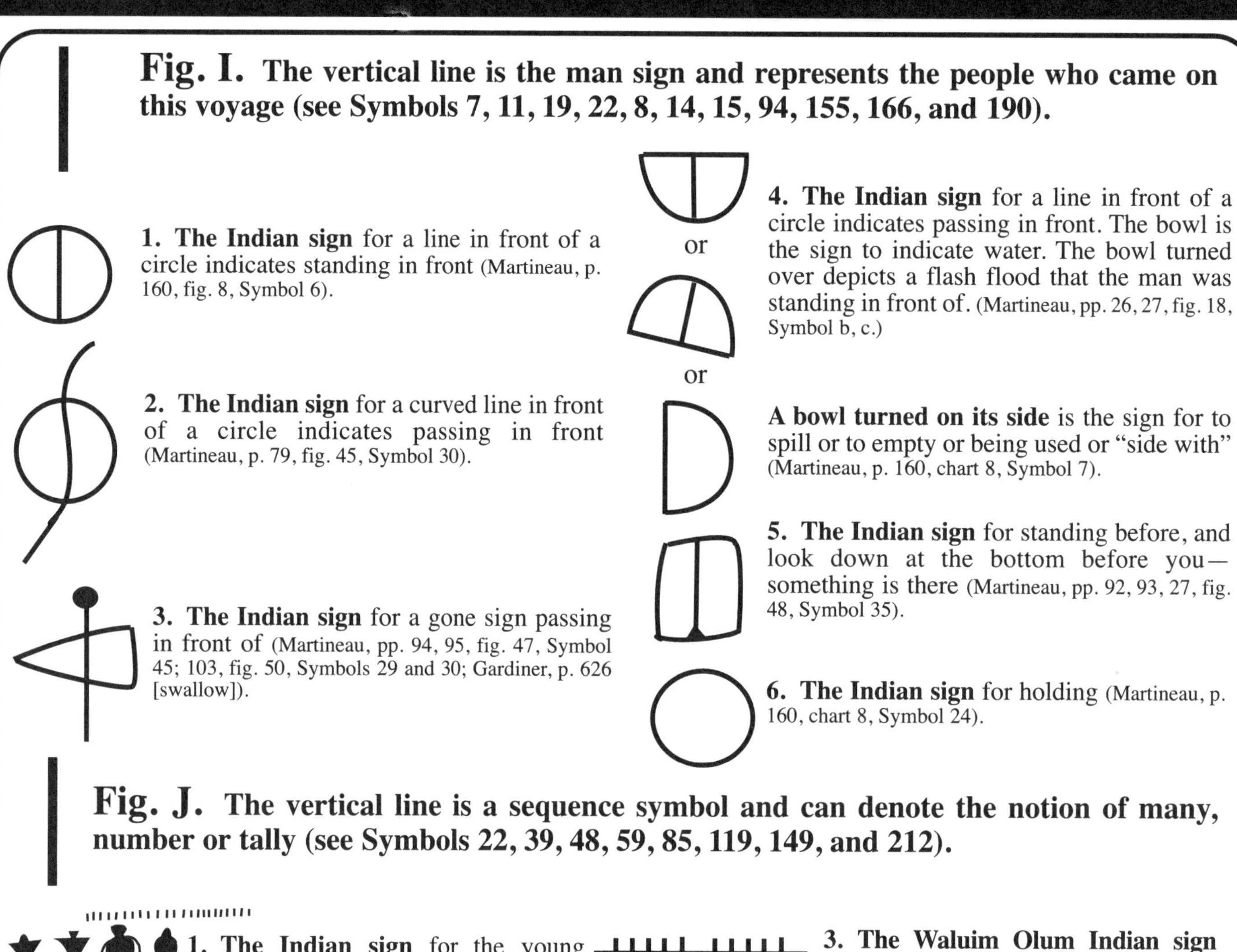

Fig. I. The vertical line is the man sign and represents the people who came on this voyage (see Symbols 7, 11, 19, 22, 8, 14, 15, 94, 155, 166, and 190).

1. The Indian sign for a line in front of a circle indicates standing in front (Martineau, p. 160, fig. 8, Symbol 6).

2. The Indian sign for a curved line in front of a circle indicates passing in front (Martineau, p. 79, fig. 45, Symbol 30).

3. The Indian sign for a gone sign passing in front of (Martineau, pp. 94, 95, fig. 47, Symbol 45; 103, fig. 50, Symbols 29 and 30; Gardiner, p. 626 [swallow]).

or

or

4. The Indian sign for a line in front of a circle indicates passing in front. The bowl is the sign to indicate water. The bowl turned over depicts a flash flood that the man was standing in front of. (Martineau, pp. 26, 27, fig. 18, Symbol b, c.)

A bowl turned on its side is the sign for to spill or to empty or being used or "side with" (Martineau, p. 160, chart 8, Symbol 7).

5. The Indian sign for standing before, and look down at the bottom before you—something is there (Martineau, pp. 92, 93, 27, fig. 48, Symbol 35).

6. The Indian sign for holding (Martineau, p. 160, chart 8, Symbol 24).

Fig. J. The vertical line is a sequence symbol and can denote the notion of many, number or tally (see Symbols 22, 39, 48, 59, 85, 119, 149, and 212).

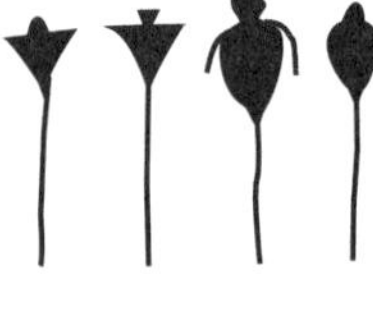

1. The Indian sign for the young children who were brought to this ceremony to be initiated into the snake clan. Their shapes indicate that they are young and new (Martineau, pp. 112, 113. fig. 57, Symbol j, k).

or

2. The Indian sign for sequence, numerous, many (see Symbols 39, 48, 59, 85, 119, 149, 212). It can depict a number of times, many days, many months or many people or much rain, depending on the other signs that it is grouped or incorporated with (Martineau, p. 112, fig. 57, Symbol k; fig. 58 b; p. 130-131, fig. 65; p. 138, chart 5 number 10).

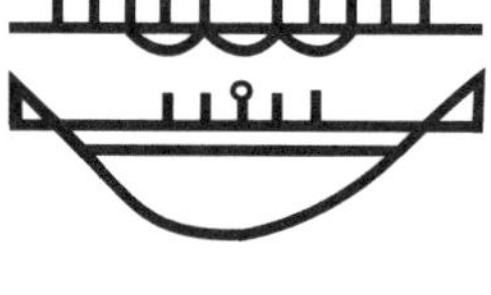

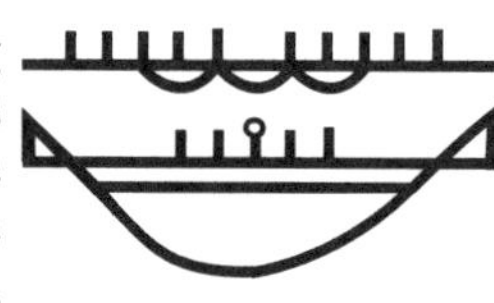

3. The Waluim Olum Indian sign for ten thousand crossing a frozen sea at night (note the human head, "gone sign," in the center on the frozen sea and the shore signs on each end of the bowl). **(Compare Symbols 22, 39, 85, 119, 149, 212.)** (Martineau, p. 172, fig. 82, Symbol b.)

4. The tribal designation of the Omahas by the Dakotas ("good on water"). "Taken from the Winter Count of Battiste Good, for the year 1744-45. The pictograph is a human head (gone sign) with cropped hair and red cheeks. It is a front view. This tribe cuts the hair short and uses red paint upon the cheeks very extensively. This character is of frequent occurrence in Battiste Good's count" (Mallery, vol. I, p. 385, fig. 504).

Fig. K. The horizontal line is a path, course, journey, trail, horizon, base line, surface (see Symbols 10, 93, 98, and 102). (Martineau, p. 160, chart 8, no. 9.)

1. A long line is the Indian movement symbol for a long journey (see Symbol 22). (Martineau, p. 160, chart 8, Symbol 15.)

2. The Indian sign for a movement to the left that is being blocked or barred. It can also depict holding firm (**see Symbols 115, 144, 178, and 182).** (Martineau, p. 160 chart 8, Symbol 15.)

3. The Indian sign for a movement to the right and left that is being blocked or barred. This sign depicts a limit or a boundary. (Martineau, p. 75, fig. 43, Symbols 12; 103, fig. 50, Symbols 29 and 30.)

4. The Indian sign for a movement to the right and left and has penetrated two barrier signs to depict the notion to "cross over" (**see Symbols 22, 26, 32, 39, 119, 42, 87, 104, 149, 178, 182, and 212**).

5. The Indian sign for cross above the surface or cross below the surface. The vertical line is a motion sign symbolizing an upward or downward direction. The two horizontal lines depict swept clean and nothing there, and can also denote the water surface **(see Symbols 59 and 190).**

6. The Zuni Indian sign for dragonfly. It is a symbol for water, fertility and abundance" (the tree of life). The vertical line is the motion sign and depicts "gone." It is crossed above the swept clean, nothing there, horizontal lines to depict "he is risen" (Bertha Dutton and Caroline Olin, *Myths and Legends of the Indians of the Southwest* [Santa Barbara:Bellerophon Books, 1978], 10) ; Bahti, p 3).

7. The Indian sign "not turning aside" (see Symbols 47 and 49). (Martineau, p. 160, chart 8, no. 11.)

8. The Indian sign "turned." (As you can see, it is important to draw these signs accurately. To round off a corner will change the meaning of the sign.) (Martineau, p. 160, chart 8, no. 16.)

9. The Indian sign "open," light, day, "to receive" (see Symbols 101, 152). This symbol is a broken base line or surface. (Martineau, p. 152, chart 6, no. 7; 110-111, fig. 56.)

10. The Indian zig-zag sign depicts the notion of lightning and fire (see Symbol 188). It is a broken vertical motion sign denoting the idea of quick or lightning fast. This symbol is representative of the God of glory, whose countenance is like fire. He is described as a fiery, flying, plumed, lightning deity who is credited with being the creator of heaven and earth (see Numbers 21:6-9; John 3:14-16; Job 41:10-34; Helaman 8:13-15). He is also known as the great white brother who has a beard and blue eyes and is known from North America all the way down into Central and South America and among the Hawaiian Islands and New Zealand. The Aztec and Toltec called him Quetzalcoatl; the Hopi called him Palolokong (Sotuhnang and Pahana); the Mayan called him Kukukcan; the Incas called him Verochocha; the Maori called him Titi kaka or Illa Tiki. (J. Eric S. Thompson, *The Rise and Fall of Maya Civilization* [Norman: University of Oklahoma Press, 1966], 122); Janake Highwater, *Arts of the Indian Americas* [New York: Harper & Row, 1983), 84; Barton Wright, *Hopi Kachinas* [Flagstaff: Northland Press, 1977] 116, 118; Bahti, page 41, 44).

11. An Akkadian sign for branch (tree of life). (Mallery, vol. II, p. 663, fig 1080, Symbol h).

12. An Indian and Akkadian sign for hand and stick (holding firm). Cypriote *ta*, apparently a causative preflex, like the Egyptian determinative; Chinese *ta*, "beat" (Mallery, Vol. II, p. 663, fig 1080, Symbol e; Martineau, p. 160, chart 8, no. 15).

13. An Egyptian sign for path, course. (Budge, p. 124, [Tu]).

14. An Egyptian sign for path, course, turn, transit, go round, circle, circulate. (Gardiner, p. 563, wdb, p. 466, F-47).

Symbol Reference

Fig. L. The Indian sign for crossed [paths crossing], within, star, place of emergence, four cardinal directions, young, renewal (see Symbols 8, 108, 136, and 155).

1. The Indian sign for "going toward." (Mallery, p. 331, fig. 438, Hunting notices.)

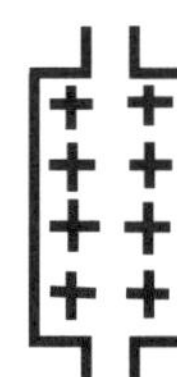

2. The Ojibwa Indian crosses represent the persons present. "They are sitting in a row." Mide lodge; Mide sitting around. (Mallery, p. 242.)

3. The Sioux Indian crosses representing arrows which are fired across the water at the opposing party. In Battiste Good's Winter Count, 1836-1837, an encounter is represented between two tribes, separated by the banks of a river, from which arrows are fired across the water at the opposing party. The vertical lines represent the banks (opposing parties), while the opposing arrows denote a fight or an encounter. (Mallery, vol. II, p. 598, fig. 929.)

4. The Indian crosses represent the notion "to cross over" (morning star). Two positions or worlds being bridged.

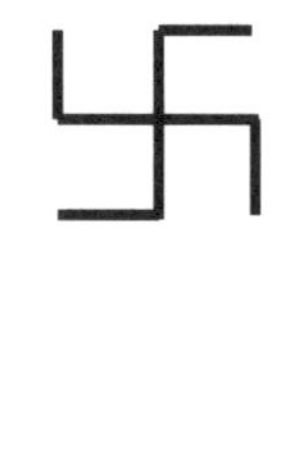

5. The Indian crosses representing the four cardinal points or the migration pattern." The Rev. Samuel Beal, rector of Flastone, North Tyrone, professor of Chinese in University College, London, writes: "Now, the earliest symbol of the earth was a plain cross, denoting the four cardinal points; hence we have the word chaturanta, the four sides, both in Pali and Sanskrit, for the earth; and on the Nestorian tablet, found at Siganfu some years ago, the mode of saying "God created the earth" is simply this; "God created the + ." (Mallery, Vol. II, p. 732; Waters, pp. 113, 114.)

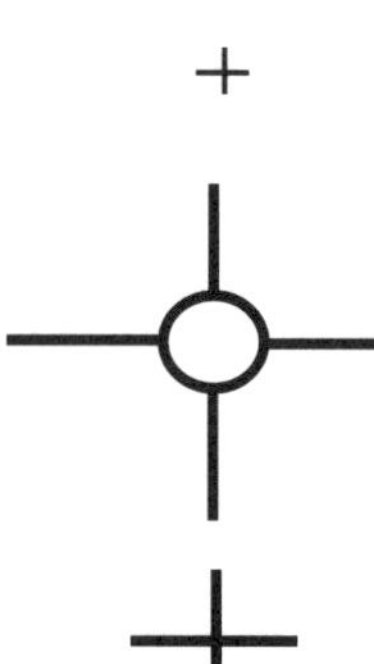

6. The Indian cross representing the four cardinal points, the Sun and a star" (Waters, p. 33, fig. 6 and 7).

or

7. The Hopi cross representing the place of Emergence. "The hole myth and meaning of the Emergence is expressed by one symbol known to the Hopis as the Mother Earth symbol. There are two forms, the square and the circular...the symbol is commonly known as Tapuat [Mother and Child]. The square type represents spiritual rebirth from one world to the succeeding one, as symbolized by the Emergence itself. In this drawing the straight line emerging from the entrance is not connected with the maze. Its two ends symbolize the two stages of life: the unborn child within the womb of Mother Earth and the child after it is born, the line symbolizing the umbilical cord and the path of Emergence. Turning the drawing so that the line stands vertical, at the top of the page, you will see that the lower end is embraced by the U-shaped arm of the maze. The inside lines represent the fetal membranes which enfold the child within the womb, and the outside lines the mother's arms which hold it later."

"The circular type differs slightly in design and meaning. The center line at the entrance is directly connected with the maze, and the center of the cross it forms symbolizes the Sun Father, the giver of life. Within the maze, lines end at four points. All the lines and passages within the maze form the universal plan of the Creator which man must follow on his Road of Life; and the four points represent the cardinal or directional points embraced within this universal plan of life. "Double security" or rebirth to one who follows the plan is guaranteed, as shown by the same enfoldment of the child by the mother. The additional meaning this circular type offers is that it also symbolizes the concentric boundaries of the land traditionally claimed by the Hopis, who have secret shrines planted along them. During Wuwuchim and other ceremonies the priest make four circuits around the village to reclaim this earth ceremonially in accordance with the universal plan."

"A structural parallel to this Mother and Child symbol is the kiva, itself the Earth Mother. The sipapuni, the small hole in the floor, represents the womb, the Place of Emergence from the preceding world; and the ladder leading out through the roof for another Emergence to the succeeding world is the umbilical cord" (Waters, p. 23, 24, fig. 1).

8. The Egyptian sign for within, in, or among (Budge, pp. 11, 12, 16, 22).

Fig. M. (The cross continued.) The Indian sign for crossed [paths crossing], within, star, place of Emergence, four cardinal directions, young, renewal and fertility (see Symbols 8, 108, 136, and 155).

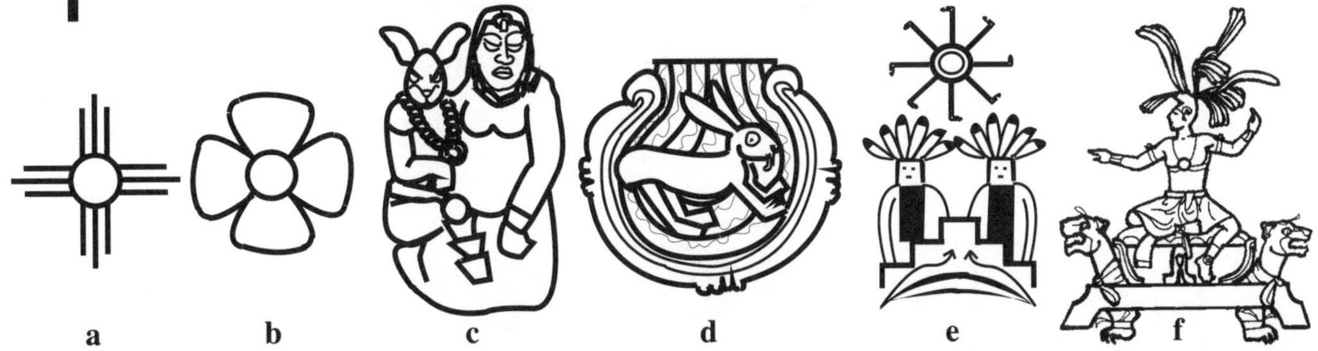

1. The Indian cross symbolizing renewal (the cross, the lotus and the rabbit are all basically the same symbol). (a) The Indian sign for the rising sun. (b) A lotus flower cross depicting rebirth and renewal. (c) Wife of the sun, the Maya moon goddess, Ixchel, patroness of fertility, from Jaina Island, of Yucatan, and takes a rabbit for her partner. (d) From a Mexican codices, a rabbit in the womb of a woman depicts birth, renewal, and to come into being. (e) This sign symbolizes the place of emergence; the rising and the renewal of the sun. It was used by the Tewa Indians of San Ildefonso to depict the emergence myth; it is a lightning and rainbow design. (f) Two guardian lions at the place of the rising sun at Palenque. Panel of "The Temple of the Beautiful Relief" (or Temple of the Lion) according to Waldeck. This great stucco relief received great renown over a century ago when he copied and published it. It has since been destroyed; only a part of the seat and one of the claws of the lion have survived. (a) L. Taylor Hansen, *He Walked the Americas* [Amherst: Amherst Press, 1963], 168; see also Budge,vol. I, p. 21, aaru; 130, Ari, Arit. (b) In the book *Before The Earth and Tales of the Beginning* by Natalia Belting, she wrote, "In the beginning there was only water and a lotus leaf floating upon it"; In the *Pyramid Texts*, Nefer-tem is called "the Lotus flower at the nose of Ra." (see *Abydos, Holy City Of Ancient Egypt*, Omm Sety and Hanny Elzeini, p. 259. (c) *National Geographic*, "The Maya, Guatemala" by Howard LaFay December 1975, p. 743). (d) Maria Sten, *The Mexican Codices and Their Extraordinary History*, [Mexico: Ediciones Lara, 1974], 35. (e) see Dalton and Olin. (f) see Thompson, p. 208, pl. 18.

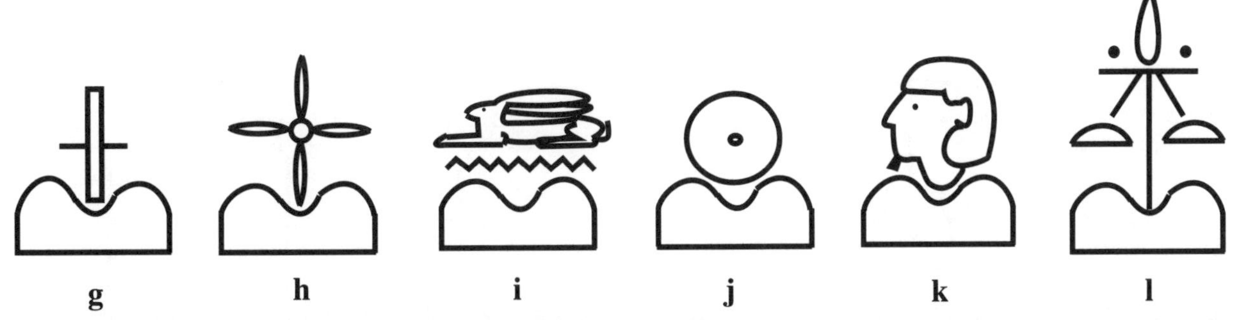

2. The Egyptian cross for renew. These symbols all give the idea of renew, sunrise, east, come into being, rebirth, resurrection, rejuvenate, cross above, emerge, or some closely connected notion. (g) Be young. To open. (h) A lotus flower, the symbol of rebirth. (i) Be, exist, to open, show oneself, come forth, renew. (j) "Sun rising over mountain, horizon, the place in the sky where the sun rises." (k) Rebirth (Nefertum, whose name means, "lotus"). (l) East, eastern horizon. The place of emergence of the sun. (g) Gardiner, p. 462, F-10; p. 484, M-42; Budge, Vol. I, p. 34, aun,aun-ra, aun her. (h) Richard Patrick, *All Color Book of Egyptian Mythology* [London: Octopus Books, 1972], plate 79; Gardiner, p. 484, M-42; Budge, Vol. I, p. 34, aun, aun-ra, aun her. (i) Gardiner, p. 461, E-34; p. 484, M-42; p. 569, wnn, exist; p. 626, there, is; Budge. Vol. I, p. 34, aun, aun her; p. 166, un, unn. (j) Gardiner, p. 489, N-27; Budge, Vol. I, p. 34, aun aun-ra, aun her. (k) Gardiner, p. 519, U-27; Patrick, plate 10; Budge, Vol. I, p. 828, tepi ta, Tepi tu, Tepitu-f. (l) Budge, Vol. I, p. cxxv, symbol 43, p. cv, 55.

Fig. N. The Indian sign for cross above the surface into the sky (heaven) or to come forth from below the surface. The vertical line is a motion sign and symbolizes an upward direction. It crosses above the horizontal line, which is the symbol for surface **(see Symbols 15, 31, 45, 52, 57, 94, 144, 186, 190, and 200).**

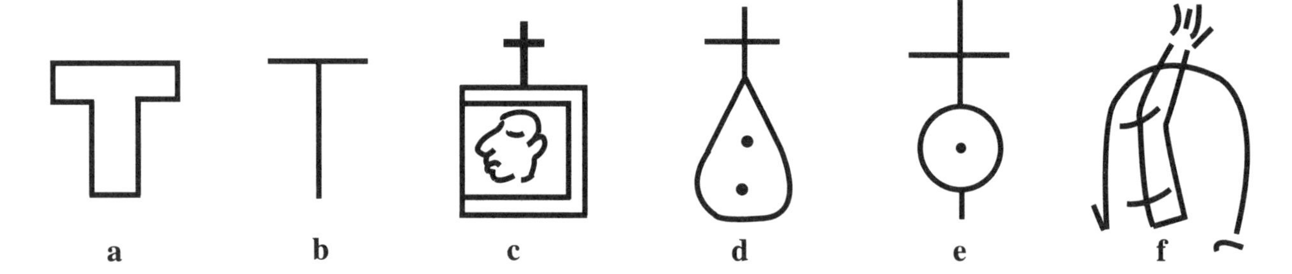

1. The Indian sign. (a) and (b) the door of the east horizon, the place of emergence of the sun with the notion of "at the east door." The symbol of the returning sun god, the place of emergence, the notion of "at the door" **(see 7, 90, 168, and 184).** (c) the god Quetzalcoatl (Kukulcan) and the sign of the tree of life, a symbol of renewal of the dead body. The return of the "sun god." The sign depicting crossing from beneath the surface to above the surface. Conveys the notion of renewal, joy, take pleasure, etc. (d) The whites. (e) The arrival of the white man. (f) A spirit having the ability to reach through the walls of his dwelling (coming forth from below the surface). (a) and (b) Waters, p. 130, fig. 54; see also *The Rise and Fall of Maya Civilization,* J. Eric S. Thompson, p. 131, fig. 13-a. (c) A detail from a pre-colombian Mexican Codex in Alexander von Humboldt's collection of codices which are in Germany. (d) Martineau, p. 139, Chart 5, no. 12, [Delaware]. (e) Martineau, p. 172, fig. 82). (f) Martineau, pp. 114, 115, fig. 59, Symbol c).

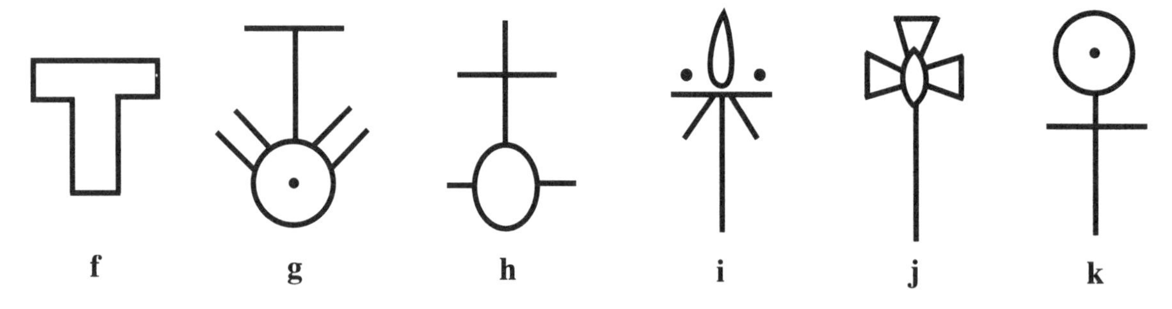

2. The Egyptian sign for "the sun (Ra or Osiris or a human soul) is at the door" or some closely connected notion. (f) door way, portal. (g) Is Ra (sun) shining at the door (h) is a kind of vessel [for milk] (Coming forth from). (i) The place of emergence of the sun with a flame or fire (soul) with the notion of "east," the left, "eastern". (j) Rising flame or fire [?], with the notion of renew, joy, take pleasure, ask, etc. (k) The sun Ra (The Creater god) is risen. (f) Budge, vol. I, p. 25, (aakhutiu); p. 88, (Asar-Taiti). (g) Budge, vol. I, p. 474, heb. (unguent used on festive occasions); p. 158, (uba, and uba-t). (h) Budge, vol. I, p. 91 Astes (one of the Company of Thoth), 127, Ankhus. (i) Budge, vol. 1, p. 18, (aabt, aabti). (j) Gardiner, p. 500, Q-7,543, Aa-27, 606, 614, 616. (k) Budge, vol. I, p. 384, (nehbt, the name of a ceremonial scepter).

Fig. O. The Indian sign for "the sun gone down" or "cross below the surface" or some closely connected notion. The vertical line is a motion sign and symbolizes a downward direction. It crosses below the horizontal line which is the symbol for surface **(see Symbols 7, 14, 22, 36, 57, 119, 149, 153, and 201).**

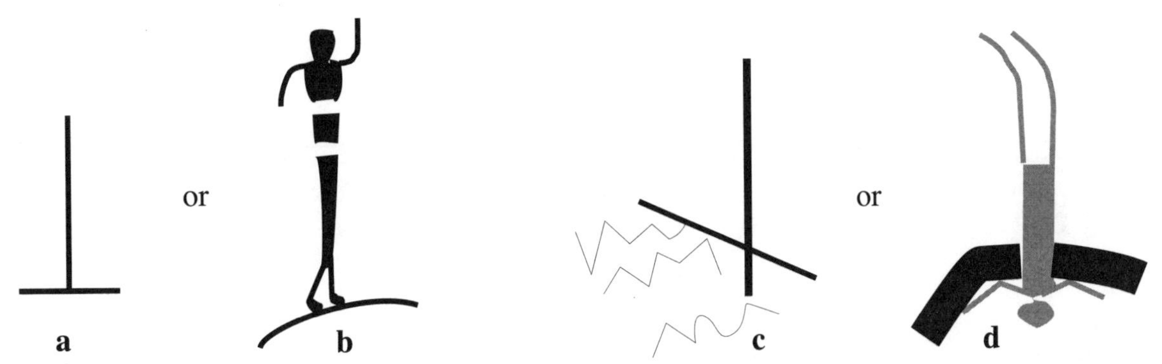

1. The Indian sign. (a) The Indian sign for standing on the surface **(see Symbols 54, 122, 185, 203, and 209).** (b) A man stomping on the sounding board over the sipapu. (c) A Navajo sign for "and they were gone from sight" (they went under the water surface). (d) The Kiowa sign for a dead man lying upside down in the water. (a) Martineau, pp. 116, 117, fig. 60, Symbol k, l). (b) Martineau, pp., 112, 113, fig. 57, Symbol c). (c) Martineau, p. 102, Fig. 50, Symbols 29, 30). (d) Martineau, p. 112, 113, Fig. 57, Symbol c).

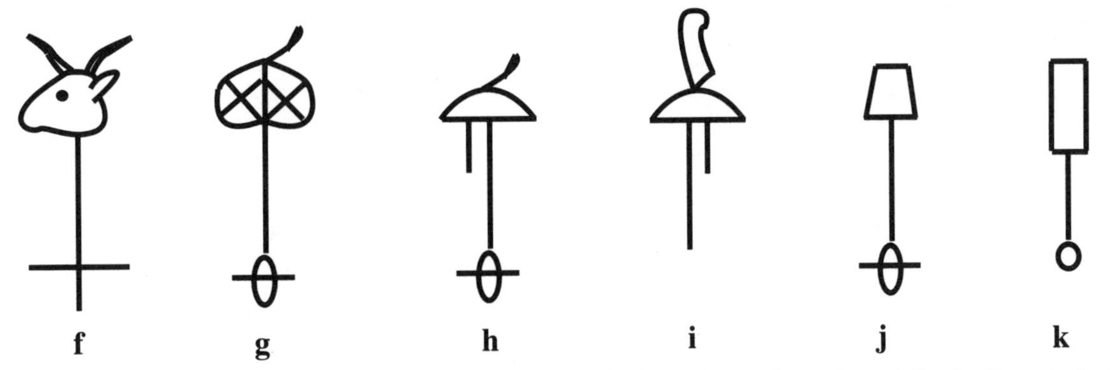

2. The Egyptian head and neck (throat) with the cross below the surface sign at the bottom to indicate a course crossing beneath a base line (surface). These symbols all depict the idea to swallow, drill (be submerged) or some closely connected notion. (f) is the head and neck [throat] of some animal, and depicts the idea of swallow. (g) A stone-worker's drill (being used to bore a hole), weighted at the top with stones. The drill bit is shown penetrating the surface to depict being used to bore a hole. (h) A repeat of the last sign with three variations. At the top the drill, it is weighted by an abbreviation of the Egyptian emblem of the west and is turned in the opposite direction, and is without the feather (it is the tool of a craftsman). (i) An Egyptian emblem to denote the West and related words, right, right-hand, side (the place where the sun goes down), etc. (j) Is the emblem of a drill being used to bore a hole in a bead, and when used with other ideograms, it denotes the notion of open up and other derivatives. (k) The base line is absent in this symbol to denote that the drill is not being used. (f) Gardiner, p. 462, F-10. (g) Gardiner, p. 518, 519, U-24, 25. (h) Gardiner, pp. 518, 519, U-24-25. (i) Gardiner, p. 502, R-14. (j) Gardiner, p. 519. U-26. (k) Gardiner, p. 519, U-27.

Symbol Reference

Fig. P. The Indian breath sign (see Symbols 8, 125, 180, and 194).

1. The Moki Indian breath sign. (Mallery, p. 705, fig. 1165.)

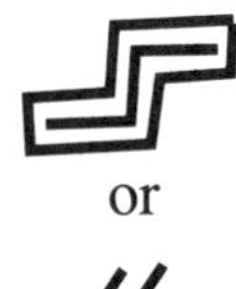

2. The Hittite sign breath, wind, Spirit. Resembles the cuneiform and Chinese emblem for "breath," "wind," "spirit." Cypriote *zo* or *ze*. Occurs as the name of a god. Akkadian *zi*, "Spirit." (Mallery p. 663, fig. 1080, Symbol v.)

Fig. Q. The Indian sign "going toward" (see Symbols 6, 19, 20, 24, 63, 66, 99, 130, 174, 183, and 207).

1. The Maori Indian Travel sign. The vertical line is the sign of man, the horizontal line is travel (Rout, p. 159).

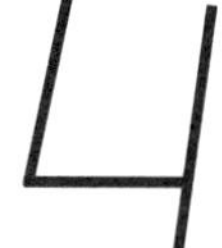

2. The Indian sign for lift, carry, or raise (see Symbols 6, 19, 24, 66, 120, 130, 170, and 207).

3. The Egyptian Post of balance, and in related verbs it gives the notion of lift, carry, or raise (Gardiner, p. 521, U-39).

Fig. R. The Indian sign of a tepee or temple pyramid with the notion of house, tomb, lord, or god (see Symbols 46, 70, 88, 118, 123 ,167, and 191).

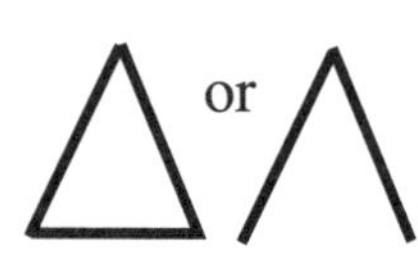

1. The Micmac Indian sign for Lord, god (the Indian signs are often abbreviated because they are considered sacred or magically dangerous). (Fell, pp. 278, 279, Psalm 114:7; Psalm 115:1,2,3.)

2. The Micmac Indian sign for the returning lord, god (the radiating lines depict shiny radiance and glory). (Fell, p. 279; Psalm 115:2.)

3. The tiara. Cypriote *Ko;* Akkadian *Ku*, "prince"; Manchu *chu*, "lord" (Mallery, vol. I, p. 663, fig. c).

4. Indian sign for "Morning star," (the returning lord, god the radiating lines depict shiny, radiance and glory). Note the face, which is the symbol of two eyes peeking out over the horizon (mouth) to depict early morning *(Toas Pueblo*, Parsons, p. 172).

5. The Egyptian pyramid sign with the notion of tomb, or lord (Gardiner, p. O-24).

Fig. S. The Indian sign for bottom, a deep hole or chamber (see Symbols 21, 24, 68, 141, and 186).

1. Indian sign for a deep bowl with just a little liquid in the bottom of it (Martineau, p. 56, fig. 36, Symbol a).

2. Indian sign for bottom, a depression, hole, or chamber (Martineau, p. 173).

3. Indian sign for beneath or under (a cliff dwelling below the mesa). (Martineau, p. 28, chart 3-A.)

4. Winnebago Indian sign for medicine animal ascending out of his hole (chamber) (Martineau, p. 28, chart 3-B).

5. Indian sign for a long-handled ladle or dipper to indicate wet (Martineau, pp. 26, 27, fig. 17-[a]; p. 92, 93 fig. 48, Symbol 39).

6. An Egyptian sign depicting (a chamber or hole?). (Budge, vol. I, p. 334, meter.)

7. An Egyptian sign depicting (a double chamber or hole?). (Budge, vol. I, p. 334, meter.)

8. An Egyptian sign depicting the bottom of anything (Budge, vol. I, p. 609, senti).

9. An Egyptian sign depicting the bottom of anything (Budge, vol. I p. 609, senti).

Fig. T. The Indian sign for bottom, a deep hole or chamber (see Symbols 66 and 144).

1. An Egyptian sign depicting (a deep chamber or hole?) (Budge, vol. I, p. 335, met-t.)

2. An Egyptian sign (A dual chamber beneath or under the surface?). (Budge, vol. I, p. 559, khent.)

Fig. U. The Indian sign for high up or on top a cover, chamber, heaven or sky (see Symbol 54). The straight vertical line can be used as a pointing finger to indicate direction, much as a modern arrow does (Martineau, pp. 17, 18 fig. 10, Symbol a).

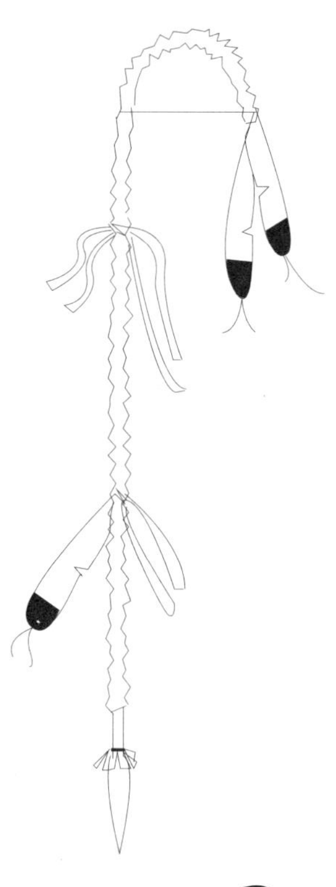

1. The Indian fur-wrapped crooked lance or staff in shorter editions might be a society emblem, and was often adorned with ribbons and eagle feathers (it was emblematic of a ladder or tree of life). "Longer ones were cut from trees by war expedition members who were chosen in the field to second the leader. The limb was cut green, bent over and tied in place, then wrapped with fur--sometimes wolf, but preferably that of otters since doing this would impart that animal's swiftness and agility to the bearer" (Thomas E. Mails, *The Mystic Warriors Of The Plains* [Garden City: Doubleday & Co., 1972], p. 362, plate 19). The straight vertical lance was symbolic of the ladder into heaven (a Jacob's ladder). The crook at the top depicted the sky over head. The crook was tied to the pole to depict the horizontal surface of the earth (Martineau, pp. 17, 18, fig. 10, Symbol a).

2. The Egyptian peasants crook [] wt. Gives the notion of flocks (note that it is not curved backward). (Gardiner, p. 509, S-39.)

3. The Egyptian crook or divine rod, scepter. Often held in the hand of the god in addition to the flail or whip and is called the hk [] which means "to rule" (Gardiner, p. 508, S-38).

Fig. V. The Indian veering or end sign to depict the notion of repel, is attached to the horizontal base line that is symbolic of a path or trail. This incorporation denotes a driving force upon the course (see Symbols 51, 111, 105, 160, and 190). (Martineau, p. 160, chart 8, Symbols 9, 22).

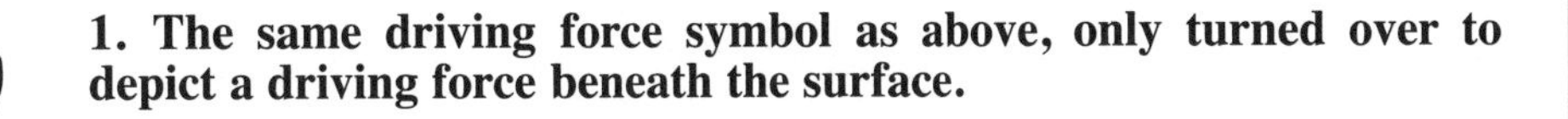

1. The same driving force symbol as above, only turned over to depict a driving force beneath the surface.

Fig. W. The Indian and Egyptian sign for circuit or to surround (see Symbols 65 and 131) (Martineau, p. 152, chart 6, Symbols 18, 22).

1. The Indian Egyptian sign for circuiting, vigorous, strong, flourishing, or reeling (see Symbol 131; Gardiner, pp. 512, T-12; 613; 625; 628).

2. The Egyptian sign for encircle, surround, or circuit (Gardiner, pp. 522, V-1, V-7, V-10).

3. The Indian and Egyptian sign for encircle, envelop, bag , bundle or circuit (Martineau, pp. 152, 112,113, fig. 57-d; Gardiner, p. 522,V-6, p. 558, rf).

Fig. X. The Micmac sign for Lord [win] (see Symbols 38, 138, and 189). (See Mallery, p. 669, fig. 1083, [win].)

1. The Maori sign for Lord. It is a variation of the male life symbol and depicts the Maori deity who led the people to Tongariro (New Zealand). (Rout, p. 160, [line 3], p. 161, [line 4], [end of line 4].)

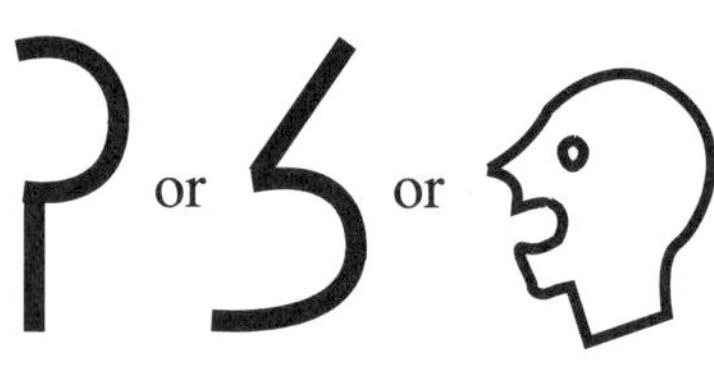

Fig. Y. The Indian sign for the mouth of a man (see Symbols 29, 94, 109, 133, 137,145, 166).

1. The Maori sign for mouth with the vertical man sign. This is one variation of the symbol depicting the sacred men who journeyed by sea to Tongariro (New Zealand) (Rout, p. 160, line 3).

2. This Maori mouth sign is another variation of the symbol to depict the sacred men who journeyed by sea to Tongariro (New Zealand). The man sign is slanted to indicate that some of these sacred men fell exhausted en route (Rout, p. 161, line 4).

3. This is the tribal designation for Assiniboin or Hohe made by the Dakota, as taken from the Winter Count of Battiste Good for the year 1709-10. "The Hohe means the voice, or, as some say, the voice of the muskox, and the device is the outline of the vocal organs, according to the Dakota concept, and represents the upper lip and roof of the mouth, the tongue, the lower lip, and chin and neck. The view is lateral, and resembles the sectional aspect of the mouth and tongue" (Mallery, p. 381, fig. 491).

The mouth of a man

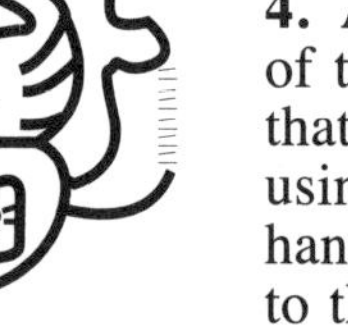

4. A glyph in which the sign-language to eat is used. "The author of the work [from which this example is taken (Seler 1904)] claims that the Indians of Huaxteca, Mexico, related to the Mayans, were still using this sign when he visited them. This gesture represents the bent hand being carried to the mouth as in the act of eating. It is identical to the sign eat as used in the United States. Note the two front teeth (two connected rectangles) near the center of this hand used to clarify this meaning. The entire glyph, then, shows a man holding food in his hand which he is either giving or receiving" (Martineau, p. 144, fig. 77 Symbol c).

Fig. Z. The Indian sign for food (see Symbols 33, 73, and 92).

Food

Or

1. **"A Mayan glyph in which the sign-language to eat is used."** "The author of the work [from which this example is taken (Seler 1904)] claims that the Indians of Huaxteca, Mexico, related to the Mayans, were still using this sign when he visited them. This gesture represents the bent hand being carried to the mouth as in the act of eating. It is identical to the sign eat as used in the United States. Note the two front teeth (two connected rectangles) near the center of this hand used to clarify this meaning. **The entire glyph, then, shows a man holding food in his hand,** which he is either giving or receiving" (Martineau, p. 144, fig. 77 Symbol c).

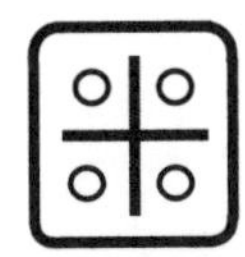

2. **This Mayan glyph indicates cut up or divided"** (Martineau, p. 144, fig. 77, Symbol d).

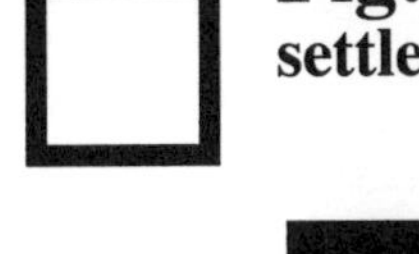

Fig. Zz. The square or rectangle is an Indian sign for object, place or settlement (see Symbols 44, 150, and 213). (Martineau, p. 160, chart 8, Symbol 21.)

1. **Indian.** "When the place sign is filled in solid it indicates that there is something there (holy) sacred, strong, bad, or encumbered and other related meanings" (Martineau, p. 116, fig. 60, Symbol f; p. 160, chart 60, Symbol 40).

2. **Hopi.** "The square is said to represent Oraibi" (Martineau, p. 116, fig. 60, Symbol f).

Fig. Zzz. The turned over "V" is an Indian sign for closed, dark, cover (see Symbols 16, 103, 148, and 154). (Martineau, p. 152, chart 6, Symbol 3.)

Fig. Zzzz. An Indian spiral sign for ascending or going up (see Symbol 135) (Martineau, p. 25, chart 3, Symbol A).

Fig. Zzzzz. An Indian spiral sign for descending or going down (see Symbols 43, 56, 62, 80, 96, and 116) (Martineau, p. 25, chart 3, Symbol A).

IDEOGRAMS OR SENSE SIGNS
SYMBOL INCORPORATIONS

Ideograms or sense-signs

Ideograms or sense-signs, are signs that convey their meaning pictorially. Thus, a , a picture of a mouth, immediately suggests to the mind, besides the notion of a mouth itself, the notions of "to eat," "to speak," or what ever you might do with a mouth. The Indian signs have, on the average, three to five meanings. Like the Egyptian, the meaning we attach to an Indian sign can vary depending on its relationship to other signs. Combining the symbols into sign incorporation causes them to take on new meanings and form complete thoughts. Like the Egyptian, the Indian signs evolved in ancient times from a formal pictorial art, into a shorthand or cursive form, the original pictorial forms of the signs no longer being clearly recognizable.

The text we are now examining is in a symbolic language. This language does not convey its message directly, but instead uses symbolism, metaphor, simile, comparisons, and other kinds of figurative language to communicate the experience. We must examine and ponder each of the symbols separately, for each symbol, used in place of words, is used as a figure of speech and depicts one subject or idea. Interestingly, in many situations, the Indian symbols seem to have Egyptian origins.

We should also mention that **the Indian pictographic system was based on their gesture speech.**

> An early explorer and archaeological researcher named Rafinesque made an important statement, which has been amply verified by the investigations of Col. Garrick Mallery, Dr. W. J. Hoffman, and Capt. W. P. Clark within the last decade: ". . . the Indian pictographic system was based on their gesture speech." It is believed that Rafinesque was the first to perceive this suggestive fact and announced it some time before 1840. Already, in *"The American Nations" (1836),* he wrote ". . . Graphic Signs correspond to these Manual Signs." Rafinesque had anticipated a leading result of his latest archaeological research. Col. Mallery, Dr. Hoffman and Capt. Clark gave Rafinesque's words great prominence, because to them, his research seemed to have been over looked by all the recent writers on Indian Gesture-speech and Sign-language.
>
> *(The Rocks Begin To Speak ,* LaVan Martineau, p. 172; *The Lenape and Their Legends,* Daniel G. Brinton, M.D., 1885; *Sign Language Among the North American Indians,* Mallery, 1881).

Ideograms or sense-signs

Sound signs:

Good examples of the Indian phonograms (sound-signs) are in the Mayan hieroglyphs, where we have been able to detect signs with a sound values which are used in spelling. There are also some good examples of sound signs in the Hopi and Micmac hieroglyphs *("Picture-Writing of the American Indians"* Garrick Mallery p. 669, fig. 1083-The Lord's Prayer in Micmac hieroglyphics).

Aholi Ka (china)

Indian Ka (china)
Spirit of the invisible forces of life *(Book of the Hopi* by Frank waters, p. 341 Glossary). Aholi, a "Germ God responsible for the germination of seeds," appears to be a resurrected form of the Hopi god Alosaka (Muyingwa the god of the afterlife) and has much in common with the Egyptian god Osiris the god of vegetation and afterlife. For after having had his throat cut, he returned back to life *(Hopi Kachinas,* Bartom Wright, p. 32).

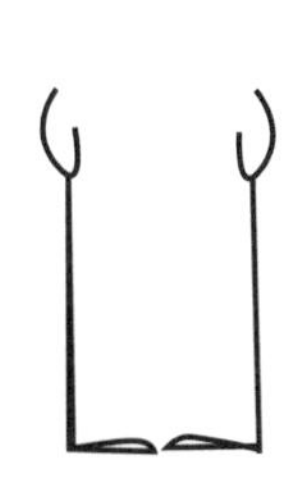

Ka

Egyptian Ka
Spirit (Spirit body). Two arms extended upwards. *("Egyptian Grammar" by Sir Alan Gardiner p. 645, General and p. 172; The Egyptian Book of The Dead,* Budge, Introduction lxi).

Original meaning of a sign and its use:

The Indian signs, like the ancient Egyptian pictorial art, are made up of Ideograms (sense signs) and convey their meaning pictorially. They signify either the actual object depicted, or else some closely connected notion.

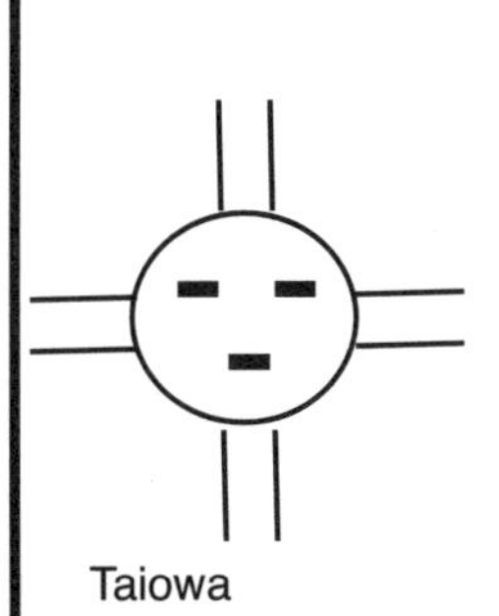

Taiowa

Indian Sun
Symbol of light, shine, and day (Hopi Sun Father Taiowa, the Divine Creator). The common Indian gesture sign for sun is when the right hand is closed, the index and thumb curved, with tips touching, thus approximating a circle, and held toward the sky, the position of the fingers of the hand forming a circle *(Picture-Writing of the American Indians,* Garrick Mallery Vol. II, p. 695, fig. 1118*)*.

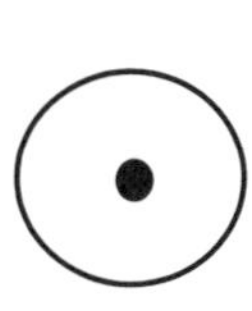

Rā

Egyptian Sun
Symbol of light and daytime (The Sun Father Ra, The Divine Creator). *(Egyptian Grammar,* Sir Alan Gardiner, p. 485,N-5; see also p. 37, Vocabulary). "Ra, a sun god described in many texts as the creator of every thing...the greatest of the deities and true father of the gods" *(Middle East-Egyptian 1981,* William Heinemann Ltt. p. 381, Published in great Britein).

Egyptian and Indian shorthand:

Out of hieroglyphic sprang a more cursive writing known to us as hieratic (Greek hieratic meaning priestly), so called because it was the usual script employed by the priests. The Indian shorthand had a similar evolution.

Maori shorthand "The Sacred Bird men"

The Maori Indian "sacred male life symbol with two beaks of bird at the base". Sons of the Sacred Bird Titi [Ka Ka], the Divine Creator (*Maori Symbolism,* Ettie A. Rout[New Zealand Law Court Reporter) New york Harcourt, Brace & Como., Inc. London: Kegan paul, Trench, Trubner & Co., Ltd. 1926, p. 159).

Hieratic "seated man"

Egyptian (hieratic) seated man with hand to mouth to depict eat, speak, feel, ex. The hieroglyphic form is also depicted below. *("Egyptian Gram- mar"* Sir Alan Gardiner, p. 442, Sect. A-2).

Hieroglyphic "seated man"

Ideograms or sense-signs

The Beautiful Relief of Palenque at "The Temple of the Lion," a Mayan Ideogram, or sense-sign, which conveys a meaning pictorially (see Symbol Reference, fig. M-f).

INDIAN PICTOGRAPHY (ROCK WRITINGS OR SENSE-SIGNS) ARE SYMBOL INCORPORATIONS

"Once this basic principle [Symbol Incorporations] was understood, . . . It was found that each of these symbols could be broken down into very common basic symbols."

LaVan Martineau, who was raised by the Paiute Indians and learned how to read their rock writings, said in his book *The Rocks Begin To Speak* the following:

> The hundreds of variations of combinations and incorporations of goats, animals, (birds), human and abstract symbols existing in rock writings point to a broad range of meaning. It was a very extensive pictography in which almost every human expression was attempted. If this were not so, or if Indian pictography had been fairly crude, these linguistic traits would instead be quite limited and not nearly so numerous. That linguistic traits do exist definitely invalidates those theories that Indian rock writings served basically as either hunting magic, hunting accounts, or art!

Martineau also said that there truly was a wide scope of expression possible in Indian pictography and that it was a highly developed writing system. The Indians were adept at expressing abstract ideas by using what we call *symbol combination* and *symbol incorporations*, or blending of signs. Symbol combinations were employed by composing symbol incorporations into a column to form phrases or sentences. Martineau said, "This type of combination, wherein symbols are only attached to other symbols . . . is accomplished by blending two (or more) symbols so that each shares part of its form with the other."

The following three pages depict a few of the many basic abstract symbols that make up the Indian vocabulary. The Indians communicated with symbol incorporations by blending abstract symbols into representational forms such as a goat, bird, or human. Martineau said that any animal, plant, or abstract could be used.

It is important also that we mention that the Indians could change the meaning of a symbol by simply filling in an outline to make it a solid or could alter or emphasize a meaning by making a thin line bold. Some of the possible new meanings would be: something there, great, strong, bad, holy, dangerous, hurt, hinder, or awkward.

Symbol Incorporations:

Abstract symbol to be blended	Representational symbol with Abstract symbol blending		
	Animal	Bird	Human
 **Fig. A** A pointing finger to indicate direction.	 1	 2	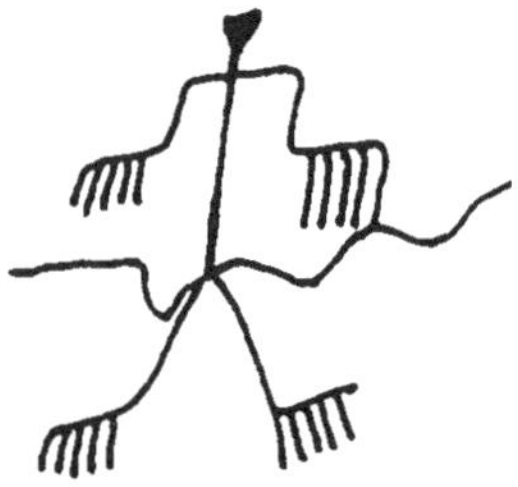 3
Fig. B place residence area object man-made	 1	 2	 3
Fig. C object place settlement man-made	 1	 2	 3
 **Fig. D** trail course journey horizon base line surface	 1	 2	 3
 **Fig. E** female sign arrowhead surrender harm	 1	 2	 3
 **Fig. F** eternal holding shield	 1	 2	 3

Symbol Incorporations:

Abstract symbol to be blended	Representational symbol with Abstract symbol blending		
	Animal	Bird	Human
 Fig. G Mouth door opening crack an objectionable area	 1	 2	 3
 Fig. H spill empty bowl on its side	 1	 2	 3
 Fig. I end end of holding end of captivity	 1	 2	 3
 Fig. J cover sky hinder repel	 1	 2	 3
 Fig. K receive opening light day	 1	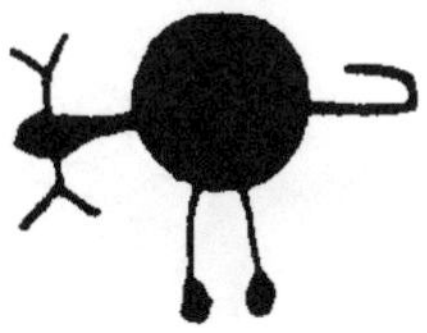 2	 3
 Fig. L closed repel destructive dark	 1	 2	 3

Symbol Incorporations:

Abstract symbol to be blended	Representational symbol with Abstract symbol blending		
	Animal	**Bird**	**Human**
Fig. M track position moccasin print here	1	2	3
Fig. N stoped waiting leaning falling	1	2	3
Fig. O within tepee peace unison	1	2	3
Fig. P arrowhead harm hurt	1	2	3
Fig. Q going up ascending	1	2	3
Fig. R bottom a depression hole chamber	1	2	3

Symbol Incorporations:

Abstract symbol to be blended	Representational symbol with Abstract symbol blending		
	Animal	Bird	Human
Fig. S canyon	1	2	3
Fig. T carry fill water	1	2	3
Fig. U hill mound kiva	1	2	3

Symbol Incorporation References

Canyon Country Prehistoric Rock Art, **by F. A. Barnes**
Fig. A-1, 261; Fig. A-3, 260; Fig. B-1, 212; Fig. B-3, 285; Fig. C-1, 155; Fig. D-1, 225; Fig. F-1, 180; Fig. F-2, 224; Fig. F-3, 134; Fig. G-1, 263; Fig. H-1, 175; Fig. I-2, 196 Fig. J-1, 30; Fig. J-3, 286; Fig. K-2, 285; Fig. L -2, 178; Fig. M-2, 199; Fig. M-3, 178; Fig. N-3, 196; Fig. O-2, 178; Fig. O-3, 176; Fig. P-3, 261; Fig. Q-2, 188; Fig. R-1, 155; Fig. S-1, 183; Fig. S-2, 196; Fig. T-1, 196; Fig. U-2, 180.

Indian Rock Art of the Southwest, **by Polly Schaafsma**
Fig. B-2, 339; Fig. C-3, 280; Fig. D-3, 29; Fig. E-1, 85; Fig. E-3, 307; Fig. H-2, 127; Fig. H-3, 147; Fig. I-1, 75; Fig. J-2, 281; Fig. K-1, 178; Fig. K-2, 285; Fig. K-3, 94; Fig. N-1, 145; Fig. N-2, 189; Fig. O-1, 16; Fig. P-l, 320; Fig. P-2, 92; Fig. P-3, 92; Fig. Q-3, 92; Fig. R-2, 123; Fig. U-1, 75; Fig. U-3, 123.

The Rocks Begin To Speak, **by LaVan Martineau**
Fig. A-2, 192; Fig. C-2, 130; Fig. E-2, 112; Fig. G-2, 132; Fig. G-3, 75; Fig. I-3, 135; Fig. K-3, 132; Fig.L-3, 132; Fig. Q-1, 183; Fig. S-3, 92; Fig. T-2, 102.

Picture-Writing of the American Indians, **Vol. 1, by Garrick Mallery**
Fig. L-1, 48; Fig. M-1, 98; Fig. T-3, 385.

MICMAC AND MAORI HIEROGLYPHICS

MICMAC INDIAN HIEROGLYPHIC SYMBOLISM

"The Micmac was an important tribe, occupying all of Nova Scotia, Cape Breton Island, Prince Edward Island, the northern part of New Brunswick, and the adjacent part of the province of Quebec, and ranging over a great part of Newfoundland" (*Picture-Writing of the American Indians,* Mallery, vol. II, 666-667).

In describing the Micmacs, Mallery wrote:

> According to Rev. Silas T. Rand, Megum is the singular form of the name which the Micmacs use for themselves. Rev. Eugene Vetromile translates 'Micmac' as 'secrets practicing men,' from the Delaware and old Abnaki word malike, 'witchcraft,' and says the name was given them on account of their numerous jugglers; but he derives Mareschite, which is an Abnaki division, from the same word and makes it identical with Micmac. The French called them Souriquois, which Vetromile translates 'good canoe men.' They were also called Acadians, from their habitat in Acadie, now Nova Scotia.
>
> The first reference in literature with regard to the spontaneous use by Indians of the characters now called the 'Micmac hieroglyphs' appears in the Jesuit Relations of the year 1652, p. 28. In the general report of that year the work of Father Gabriel Druillettes, who had been a missionary to the Abnaki (including under this term the Indians of Acadia, afterwards distinguished as Micmacs), is dwelt upon in detail. His own words, in a subordinate report, appear to have been adopted in the general report of the Father Superior, and translated, are as follows:
>
> 'Some of them wrote out their lessons in their own manner. They made use of a small piece of charcoal instead of a pen, and a piece of bark instead of paper. Their characters were novel, and so *particuliers* [individual or special] that one could not know or understand the writing of the other; that is to say, that they made use of certain marks according to their own ideas as of a local memory to preserve the points and the articles and the maxims which they had remembered. They carried away this paper with them to study their lesson in the repose of the night.'
>
> We have ourselves been witnesses of a similar fact among the Tetes-de-Boule Indians of the River St. Maurice where we had been missionaries during three years. We often saw during our instructions or explanations of the catechism that the Indians traced on pieces of bark, or other objects very singular hieroglyphs. These Indians afterward passed the larger part of the following night in studying what they had so written, and in teaching it to their children or their brothers. The rapidity with which they by this manner learnt their prayers was very astonishing.
>
> The Indians called by the Abbe Maurault the Tetes-de-Boule or Round Heads, are also known as Wood Indians, and are ascertained to have been a band of the Ojibwa, which shows a connection between the practice of the Ojibwa and that of the Micmacs, both being of the Algonquian stock, to mark on bark ideographic or other significant inscriptions which would assist them to memorize what struck them as of special interest and importance, notably religious rites (*Picture-Writing of the American Indians,* Mallery, vol. II, 666-667).

Barry Fell wrote about John Williams, an associate of his, who was searching through some documents stored in the great Widener Library of Harvard College. In the course of inquiry he consulted works in the Indian languages. Fell said:

> One day John brought me a copy of a curious document printed in New York in 1866, and included in a book on the Wabanaki Indians of Maine written by Eugene Vetromile, a priest who ministered to the Indians. This document, comprising a single sheet, was headed The Lord's Prayer in Micmac Hieroglyphs.

Fell remarked about the document:

> At first glance I perceived that about half (at least) of the hieroglyphic signs were remarkably similar to Egyptian hieroglyphs as rendered in the simpler cursive form called hieratic. (*America B.C. Ancient Settlers in the New World*, Barry Fell, 253)

Fell had reproduced in his book, on page 254, part of Psalm 115 (see also pp. 280 and 281) in the Micmac Hieroglyphs from the Non nobis Domine as composed by the Abbe Maillard circa 1738.

Psalms 115

4 Their idols are silver and gold, the work of men's hands.

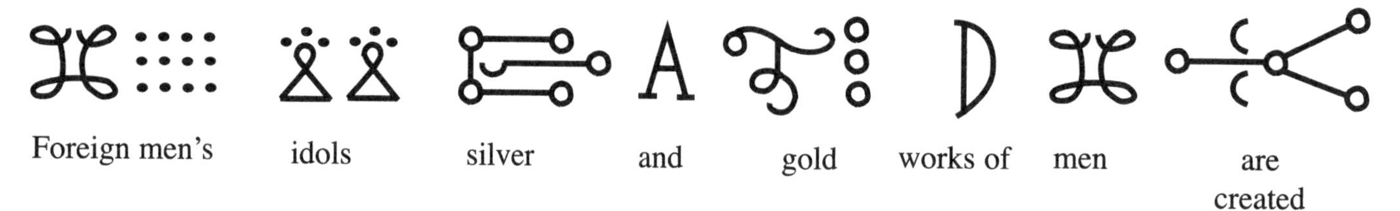

5 They have mouths, but they speak not: eyes have they, but they see not:

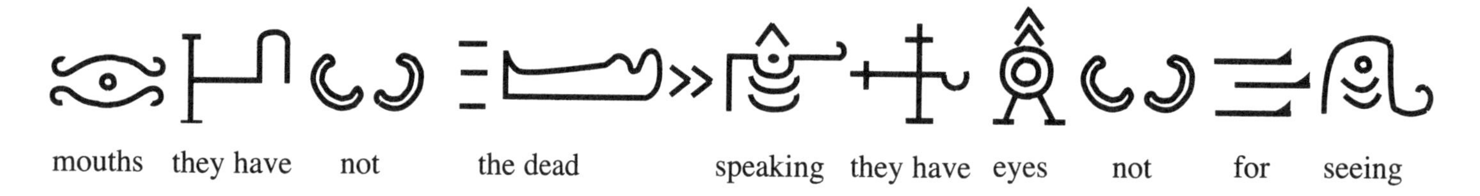

6 They have ears, but they hear not: noses have they, but they smell not:

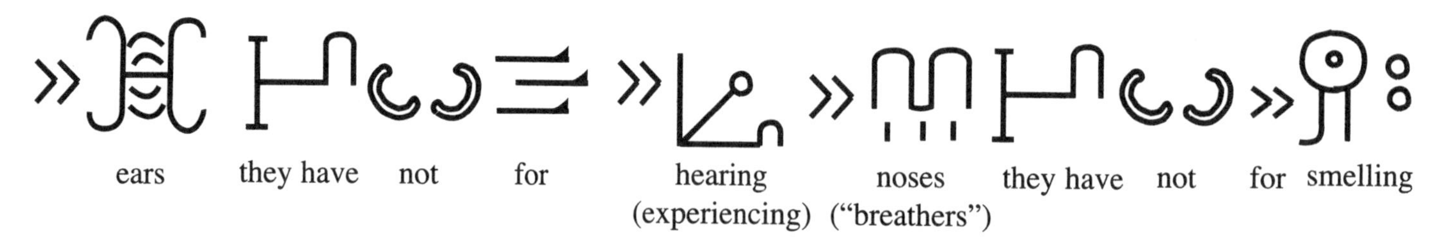

MAORI INDIAN SYMBOLISM

The following is an account of the origin, migration, and culture of the New Zealand Maori as recorded in certain Sacred Legends.

It is a report made by Ettie A. Rout (London: Harcourt, Brace & Company, 1926).

Heading

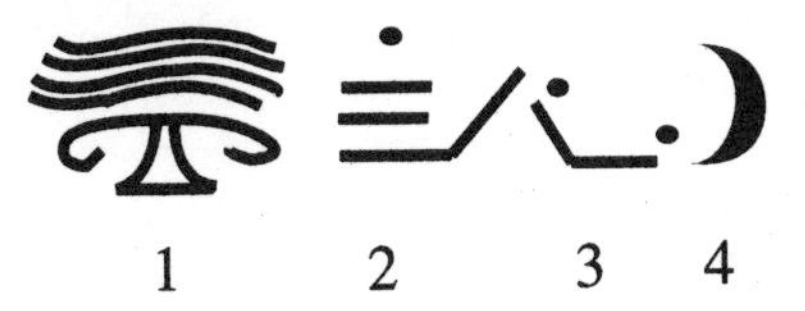

1 2 3 4

Symbol 1: A straight line is used to indicate travel. A waved line is used to indicate travel by sea. The last curve downward indicates that the journey is unfinished. The four lines here indicate four different halting places. The second sign in symbol one is the sacred male life symbol, plus two beaks at base. The sign indicates that what follows is a sacred legend. Note that the Maori would not include the word "sacred" in his translation of the script, but this would be understood by the mere fact that the legend relates to Tohu (the Divine Father) and Tiki (the Divine Son, the Seed of Eperu [Apera or Abraham]. In Maori religion Tiki is also called Te Mihaia [the Messiah]. He is accounted as the offspring of God, but a Divine Man. Tiki was supposed to have had a virgin-birth, his mother being fertilized by the Third Person in the Trinity—the Great Spirit. Tiki is the God and the Man (Rout, p. 162).
Symbol 2: The dot is the sign in script for island. The two straight parallel lines mean short voyages. The single straight line means travelling to and from; and the slanting line is half the sign of the mountain Tongariro (New Zealand). **Symbol 3:** The short slanting line is half the sign for Rarotonga (Tahiti), and the short horizontal line indicates the journey from Easter Island to Rarotonga by way of several islands. **Symbol 4:** The crescent sign represents Easter Island (the Navel of the Earth).

Line (1)

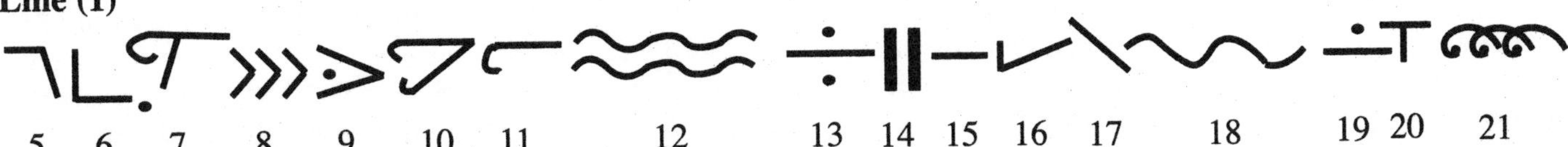

5 6 7 8 9 10 11 12 13 14 15 16 17 18 19 20 21

Symbol 5: The horizontal line is travel. The slanting line is half the sign for Rarotonga. **Symbol 6**: The vertical line is the sign of man. The horizontal line at base of vertical line indicates travel. The dot is the sign for island. **Symbol 7:** The hooked line is part of male life symbol, indicating that the voyagers were sacred men (members of the intellectual aristocracy), the Seed of Eperu (Apera or Abraham). These travellers were God's selected children "the children of God's eye," and that they were under his eye (under his direction and protection). The slanting line is half the sign of Tongariro, indicating that Tongariro (New Zealand) is the new sacred home of these godlike men. **Symbol 8:** The three triangles are parts of male life symbols, and in this form they indicate three generations. **Symbol 9:** The angular sign following is the beak of the bird (the sacred Bird Kaka, the Divine Creator, God Himself, who led the voyagers in their journey). The dot in the beak of the bird indicates the travellers who were God's selected children "the children of God's eye," and they were under his eye (under his direction and protection). **Symbols 10, 11, 12.:** These signs indicate that continuous sea voyages ultimately landed these sacred men at New Zealand. The top part of **Symbol 10** is the male life symbol. The long slanting line is the Tongariro (New Zealand); and the short slanting line is the Rarotonga (Tahiti) sign. **Symbol 11** is (only part of the sign is shown) the male life symbol, indicating that the voyage was under the direction of Sacred Men. **Symbol 12.** The wavy lines indicate a long continuous sea voyage. (There need not necessarily be only two lines, but there must be more than one to indicate more than one voyage.) **Symbol 13.** The dots are islands; the horizontal line between indicates voyaging between different islands. **Symbol 14.** The two heavy upright lines indicate that the voyagers were men. **Symbol 15.** The horizontal line at end indicates that the voyages were continuous, and were exploring expeditions leading ultimately to the place indicated in the following sign. **Symbol 16.** The first short slanting line is Rarotonga (Tahiti),and the long slanting line indicates that there was a journey from Rarotongo (Tahiti). **Symbol 17.** The next long slanting line represents Tongariro (New Zealand), indicating that voyagers reached New Zealand. **Symbol 18.** The curved line indicates by its last part pointing upwards that the voyage ended in New Zealand. **Symbol 19.** This horizontal line with dot over it indicates a voyage from an island. **Symbol 20.** This sign indicates man (men). **Symbol 21.** These last signs are three sacred male life symbols, indicating three generations during this particular voyage.

Line (2)

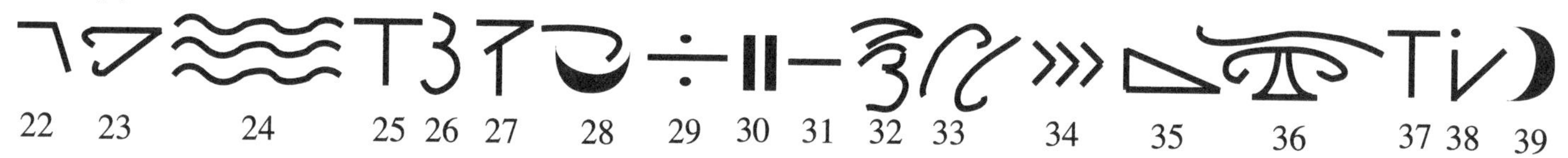

Symbols 22, 23, 24. These signs indicate a strenuous sea voyage from Rarotonga to Tongariro by these Sacred Men. **Symbol 25** is the sign for man. **Symbol 26** is a variation of male life symbol (it is the Maori symbol for Tiki, Lord or the God who lead them to Tongariro [New Zealand]). **Symbol 27** is the beak of the bird (top) and man sign (vertical line). **Symbol 28** is the crescent indicating Easter Island (the Navel of the Earth), and the sign above the crescent is the male sign indicating that this island is a Sacred Place (Tiki was supposed to have been buried at Easter Island). **Symbols 29, 30, 31** indicate sea voyages (exploring expeditions by the scientists from island to island). **Symbol 32** is the beak sign, and is the beak of the bird imposed on male life-symbol (it is this Maori bird god, the Divine Creator, that is identical to the Egyptian bird god Horus, the day Sun, who overcame death and represented the dead god Osiris. The Maori make the claim that their original home was the land of the pyramid [Assyria]. The Maori say, "Tiki is the God and the Man, and Titikaka is the country, whence sprang your brave and noble ancestors." **Symbol 33** is variations of two sacred male life symbols. Symbol 34. Three triangular marks indicating three generations. **Symbol 35.** The beak of the sacred bird God. (Symbol 32, 33, 34, 35, is a group of signs symbolizing that these Sacred Bird men reproduced in three generations, race-improvement being indicated by the sacred beak; in other words, their reproduction was in accordance with the guidance of the Sacred Bird (the Divine Creator). **Symbol 36, 37, 38, and 39** indicates that the Sacred Bird-men who had travelled to Easter Island reproduced themselves on that island.

Line (3)

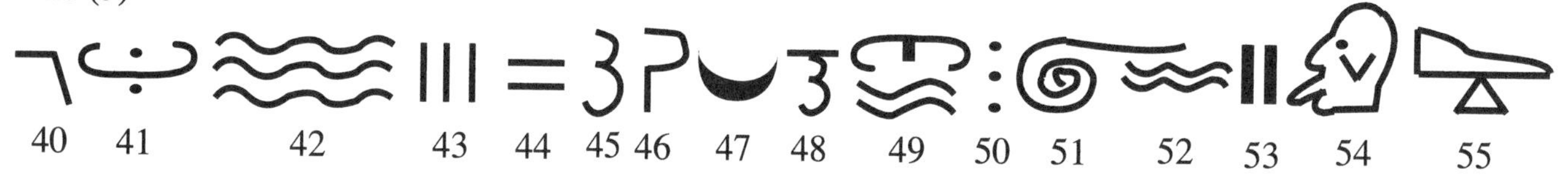

Symbols 40, 41, 42, and 43 indicates a sea-voyage to Tongariro by the fruit of the loins of three generations. indicate that the voyage was incomplete and to be continued. **Symbol 45, 46, 47, 48 and 49** indicates that the three generations were reproduced on Easter Island **Symbol 45** is a male life symbol; **Symbol 46** is the beak (mouth) and man sign (underneath the mouth). **Symbol 47** is the Easter Island sign. **Symbol 48.** The horizontal line with male life-symbol under it indicates that these Sacred Men were engaged in exploring, discovery, and research work until, **symbol 49**, the day of departure (indicated by wavy lines). The sacred male life symbol over the wavy lines indicates the re-beginning of the Great Migration to the west (Notice the vertical man sign has been made bold). **Symbol 50** is three dots to indicate the islands composing The Navel of the Earth. **Symbol 51** is a spiral and line to indicate the Beginning of this Stage of the Great Migration. **Symbol 52** The two wavy lines indicate that there were two previous stages. **Symbol 53.** The two upright lines indicate men. **Symbol 54**. The face is the sign of Eperu (or Apera or Apera-hama; Abraham), indicating that this migration was a part of the journey of the children of God in search of the Promised Land, but the triangle inside the face outline indicates that only some of these children went on this journey. The dot indicates that the travellers were God"s selected children (in Maori the words are "the children of God's eye"), and that they were under his eye—under his direction and protection. **Symbol 55**. The beak of the bird indicates that the Great Migration began in the original home of the

Sacred Bird. The Pyramid sign underneath indicates that original home was the Land of the Pyramid (Assyria) or (Egypt).

Line (4)

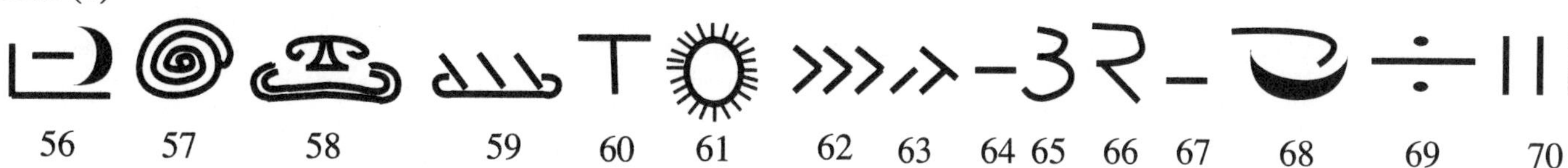

56 57 58 59 60 61 62 63 64 65 66 67 68 69 70

Symbols 56, 57, 58, 59, 60, and 61 are a group of signs indicating the journey of the Children of God (or the Children of the Sun) from the mainland to Easter Island. The vertical line in **Symbol 56** is a man; the horizontal line is the connection. (The Short horizontal line is the sign for journey. The crescent symbol is for Easter Island). **Symbol 57** is a spiral to indicate a strenuous land journey. This spiral starts with a circle and ends with a downward line, indicating a land journey. Note that this downward line at the end is joined to the inside spiral to denote hindered or strenuous. **Symbol 58:** The combination of male life symbols indicates that the travellers were sacred. **Symbol 59**: the slanting of the three lines in this symbol indicates that some of these sacred men fell exhausted en route. **Symbol 60** is the man (or men) sign. **Symbol 61** is the sign for sun, to indicate again that these travellers were children of Ra [Egyptian name for (Sun-God)]. **Symbol 62** is three generations. **Symbol 63** is two elders (the sign for elder is one slanting line with another across the top of it—derived from the man-sign). **Symbol 64:** the horizontal line indicates a journey. **Symbol 65** is a male sign and follows the journey sign to show that it was a sacred journey. **Symbol 66** is the beak (mouth) sign with the man sign joined to indicate that the journey was under the direction of the Sacred Bird (God). **Symbol 67** is a horizontal line to connect the journey with **Symbol 68,** which is the crescent indicating Easter Island; and the sign above the crescent is part of the male life-symbol, indicating that this island is a Sacred Place in the island group. **Symbol 69** is two dots and a horizontal line to indicate sea voyages between islands. **Symbol 70** is three upright lines representing three generations of the Sons of God.

71 72

The horizontal line **Symbol 71** connects these men with the sacred symbols in **Symbol 72**. Three of these sacred male life symbols here indicate the Divine Trinity, the one in the middle being the Divine Father (or Creator), the one on the left the God of Nature, and the one on the right the Great Spirit.

Line (5)

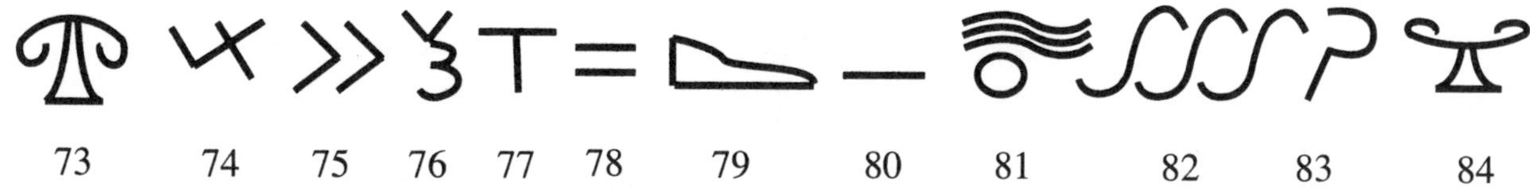

73 74 75 76 77 78 79 80 81 82 83 84

Symbol 73 is the male symbol with beaks of bird. **Symbol 74** represents the reproduction of... **Symbol 75:** the following generations. **Symbol 76** is the sign of children (V) and the sacred male Symbol under this, which indicates that the children were sacred (Sons of God). **Symbol 77** is the sign of for man (or men). **Symbols 78 and 79:** Two horizontal parallel lines followed by the sacred beak indicate that these sacred children grew into bird-men (scientists). **Symbol 80** is a straight, horizontal line to indicate a connection (travel). **Symbol 81:** The three wavy lines indicate migration by sea, and the circle under indicates a number of islands. **Symbol 82:** The three "S" signs are each made up of two male organs, indicating the hereditary nobility (the particular number of these signs does not matter—so long as more than one is used). **Symbol 83**: The beak (mouth) imposed on upright (or slanting) line indicates bird-men. **Symbol 84** is the sacred male life symbol inverted and placed over sacred beaks; this derivation of the sacred male life symbols and bird symbols indicates Woman as the Sacred House (or Mother).

Line (6)

Symbols 85 and 86 indicate a voyage from Easter Island. **Symbol 87** is the man sign and indicates the noble ancestors of the Maori. A dot following these man-signs—the first sign larger than the second indicates ancestry. **Symbol 88:** The beak (mouth) sign, placed on top of a vertical line (man-sign), indicate that these ancestors were scientists (bird men). **Symbol 89** is two male life symbols which indicate their reproduction. **Symbol 90** is the double beak sign to indicate that these noble ancestors were born in the Land of the Sacred Bird. **Symbol 91** is the sacred symbol for children or descendants. **Symbol 92** is three generation signs, indicating many generations. **Symbols 93 and 94** are two sacred male life symbols indicating that these generations were "the fruit of the loins" was the conscious reproduction of selected parents, guided by... **Symbol 95:** The beak of the bird indicates that the guide was the Sacred Bird (the Divine Creator or God Himself). **Symbol 96:** The face is the of the Divine ancestor, or Divine Father—or the Creator Himself. Tiki is his representative, that is Tiki is the Divine Son, the Seed of Eperu (Apera or Abraham).

Putting this connectedly into very brief English, it reads as follows:

The Annals by Tohu, the Son of Tiki, The Issuing from Peru to New Zealand of Our Brave and Noble Ancestors.

Now you are in New Zealand. On the wings of the wind you came from Tahiti. During the sea-voyage the canoes were paddled with the greatest difficulty and hardship, aided by the God of Might (Tohu), and thus you reached Rapa-nui from Rapa-iti, and Rapa-iti from Easter Island. There (at Easter Island) rest the sons of Eperu who came from Hawaiki—the ancestral home of our House (that is, of the House of Arawa). Tiki is the God and the Man, and Titikaka is the country, whence sprang your brave and noble ancestors.

This heading is really the 'text' from which a 'sermon' to the people would be preached somewhat as follows:

Tongariro is the land-mark of the New Zealand home of the Maori race. It is a most sacred mountain. It is named after Rarotonga, the last halting-place of the Maori in their Migration Westward. These Maori Voyagers were our immediate forefathers: we live in them and they in us: we are their descendants: the fruit of their loins. We have come far across the sea. We have suffered many hardships and great tribulations; only by the most strenuous effort did we reach New Zealand (*Te-Ika-a-Maui* is the Maori name for New Zealand, meaning the Stone Fish of the Sea).

It is but fitting and natural that we should endure and survive. We migrated here to secure freedom of thought, peace of mind, happiness of life. These were all denied to us at Titikaka: therefore we resolved to migrate still further westwards to the land of the setting sun. None joined in this great adventure but the free and the brave: nobles and the children of nobles. Scientists and leaders were they all—far in advance of the general community in knowledge, physique, intellect and courage. Nevertheless, through their ignorance and bigotry, the People rejected the teaching of these Elders, who were the fruit of the loins of Tiki: they were the Children of God, but the Sons of Man born of Woman. Their origin and birth are commemorated by the sacred ornament, the Tiki. Therefore should this ornament always be respected and venerated; it should call to mind not only the land we left behind: our beloved home at Titikaka: but also these great and wonderful forefathers who struggled first over the mountain passes day after day from Titikaka till the Western Coasts of Peru were finally reached. There we all assembled and from there we departed.

After a long and most exhausting journey by sea the hardest test any of the Maori race has undergone—we reached land—the land we called The Navel of the Earth. Worn and disabled, long we rested there. Our scientists studied this land and found it dry and barren, and proved that it was only a small island. Our voyage had not ended. We must go still further westward. Then came another long and trying sea-voyage till we reached Rapa-iti, where again we rested. Again it became clear that our migration was not yet complete. We prepared for another voyage, and soon reached Rapa-nui. Resting there for some time, we realized once more that we had failed to reach the Promised Land. Again we set forth, and this time reached Rarotonga—a large group of islands in the midst of the ocean. Unfortunately there a quarrel arose, and one party of nobles sailed northward: we came southward on the advice of our scientists and navigators who had searched the seas to the west. Thus ultimately did we reach Te-Ika-a-Maui.

Always had we struggled towards the land of the setting sun, the Promised Land, the Land of Paradise, the Golden Land where the forest was evergreen—the land where there were no beasts of prey, no snakes, no poisonous and dangerous creatures, the land where happiness and health were within the reach of all of us.

Consider then what you have all passed through. Consider the tribulations and dangers you have endured and overcome. Consider your duty to the past, to the present, to the future. You were born innocent: you must die innocent. But at present some of you are sinful: you are failing to improve yourselves: you are even failing to maintain your own original standards. Reform yourselves. Mend your ways. Remember—*By being unfit to live you will render your selves unfit to die.*

These are only three of the Sacred Legends of the New Zealand Maori—namely, those concerning the Great Migration Westwards. The Maori scientists and elders recognized that these Sacred Legends were ancient mythology. The persons in the Trinity were given different names at different times, as were the human representatives of The Messiah. The People regarded the Sacred Legends as embodying actual historical facts: the Elders regarded the Sacred Legends as embodying fundamental ethical principles.

SELECT BIBLIOGRAPHY

BOOKS

Barnes, F.A. *Prehistoric Rock Art.* Salt Lake City: Wasatch Publishers, Inc., 1982.

Bahti, Tom. *Southwestern Indian Ceremonials.* Las Vegas: KC Publications, 1970.

Berrett, William Edwin. *The Restored Church A Brief History of the Growth and Doctrines of the Church of Jesus Christ of Latter-day Saints.* Salt Lake City: Deseret Book Company, 1958.

Budge, E. A.Wallis. *An Egyptian Hieroglyphic Dictionary.* Vols. 1 & 2, New York: Dover Publications, Inc., 1978.

——— *The Egyptian Book of The Dead.* New York: Dover Publications, Inc., 1967.

Chessman, Paul R. *These Early Americans.* Salt Lake City: Deseret Book Company, 1974.

Church Educational System. *The Life and Teachings of Jesus Christ.* Salt Lake City: The Church of Jesus Christ of Latter-day Saints, 1978, 1979.

Cook, Lyndon. *David Whitmer Interviews.* Grandin Book Company, 1993.

Encyclopedia of Mormonism. Vol. 1, New York: Macmillan Publishing Company, 1992.

Fell, Barry. *America B.C.* New York: Pocket Books, 1976.

Gardiner, Sir Alan. *Egyptian Grammar.* Oxford: Friffith Institute Ashmolean Museum, 1976.

Hansen, L. Taylor, *He Walked the Americas.* Amherst: Amherst Press, 1963.

Mails, Thomas E.*The Mystic Warriors Of The Plains* . Garden City: Doubleday & Co., 1972.

Mallery, Garrick. *Picture-Writing of the American Indians.* Vols. 1 & 2, New York: Dover Publications, Inc., 1972.

Martineau, LaVan. *The Rocks Begin To Speak.* Las Vegas: KC Publications, 1976.

Maxwell, Neal A. *Plain and Precious Things.* Salt Lake City: Desert Book, 1983.

——— *My Kingdom Shall Roll Forth.* Salt Lake City: The Church of Jesus Christ of Latter-day Saints, 1979.

Nibley, Hugh. *Since Cumorah.* Salt Lake City: Deseret Book Company, 1976.

——— *The Collected Works of Hugh Nibley: Volume 5 The Book of Mormon.* Edited by John W. Welch, with Darrell L. Matthews and Stephen R. Callister. Salt Lake City: Desert Book Company and Provo: Foundation for Ancient Research and Mormon Studies, 1988.

Patrick, Richard. *All Color Book of Egyptian Mythology.* London: Octopus Books, 1972

Peterson, H. Donl. *The Story of The Book of Abraham.* Salt Lake City: Deseret Book Company, 1995.

Roberts, B. H. *Comprehensive History of the Church.* Vol. 1, Salt Lake City: Deseret Book Company, 1949.

Rout, Ettie A. *Maori Symbolism* . London: Harcourt, Brace & Company, 1926.

Todd, Jay M. *The Saga of the Book of Abraham.* Salt Lake City: 1969.

Smith, Lucy Mack. *History of the Prophet Joseph Smith.* Salt Lake City: 1954.

——— *Messenger and Advocate.* 1834-35.

Sorenson, John L. *An Ancient American Setting For The Book Of Mormon* . Salt Lake City: Deseret Book Company, 1985

Sschaafsma, Polly. *Indian Rock Art of the Southwest.* Santa Fe: University of New Mexico Press, 1980.

Stevenson, Edward. *Reminiscences of the Prophet Joseph,* Salt Lake City, 1893.

Waters, Frank. *The Book of the Hopi.* Harrisonburg: R.R. Donnelley & Sons Company, 1963.

Webb, R. C. *Joseph Smith as a Translator.* Salt Lake City: The Deseret News Press, 1936.

Widtsoe, John A. & Harris, Franklin S. Jr. *Seven Claims of the Book of Mormon.* Independence: Press of Zion's Printing and Publishing Company, 1937.

Wright, Barton. *Hopi Kachinas.* Flagstaff: Northland Press, 1977.

ARTICLES

Barker, James L. "The Language fo the Book of Mormon," *The Improvement Era,* June 1960.

Benson, Ezra Taft. "The Book of Mormon—Keystone of our Religion," *Ensign,* Nov. 1986.

Crowley, Ariel L. "The Anthon Transcript," *Improvement Era,* Jan-Mar 1942.

F.A.R.M.S. Staff. "Martin Harris' Visit With Charles Anthon," STF-90.

Kimball, Stanley B. "The Anthon Transcript: People, Primary Sources, and Problems," *BYU Studies,* 10, 1970.

——— "Charles Anthon And The Egyptian Language," *The Improvement Era,* October, 1960.

——— "I Cannot Read a Sealed Book," Faculty History Department, The City College, New York: *The Improvement Era,* Feb. 1957.

LaFay, Howard. "The Maya, Guatemala," *National Geographic,* Dec. 1975.

Maxwell, Neal A. "True Believers in Christ," 1980 *Devotional Speeches of the Year.* BYU, 1981, pp. 134-40.

Packer, Boyd K. *Conference Report,* Oct. 1982.

Welch, John W. and Tim Rathbone. "The Translation of the Book of Mormon: Basic Historical Information," Provo, Utah: F.A.R.M.S., 1986.

INDEX